Dishonoured and Unheard

Christian Women and Domestic Violence

Daphne Marsden

Dishonoured and Unheard
Christian Women and Domestic Violence

Daphne Marsden

Auckland: 2018

Dishonoured and Unheard: Christian Women and Domestic Violence

Daphne Marsden

Archer Press

P.O. Box 12149

Penrose

Auckland 1061

New Zealand

Archer PRESS

© 2018

ISBN: 978-0-473-43721-3

"The first time that he hit me I was on the bed and he was slapping my face, side to side, hurting me. I just lay there and let him do it to me. Where did that come from?! I've not a clue. I didn't know it was abuse. That was early in our marriage; I was married to him for many years. Covenant is something to be taken seriously. I didn't think God ever broke covenants, so if we made a covenant with God, then we shouldn't break it either. Which sort of takes my mind down the road to - well, how bad is divorce then? I thought I had to keep forgiving him."

Mary invites us into her world as a Christian woman experiencing domestic abuse. It is not easy for women like Mary to find well informed and safe spiritual care. However, in this book women like Mary, along with pastors, counsellors, theology students, and friends will find guidance grounded in scripture. Forgiveness, marriage as a covenant, headship, and submission are explored. Drawing from women's stories, researchers, and biblical scholars this book offers a compassionate response to Christian women living with and recovering from domestic violence.

With gratitude and love I dedicate this book to the memory of the late Dr Catherine Clark Kroeger (1925-2011). Like many others, I am grateful for her courage, her superior biblical scholarship, her hospitality, and her advocacy.

Endorsements

"This is an extremely important book for the church. The helpful way Daphne brings together the Bible and theology with the difficult realities of life means this will become an essential resource for me in the training of people for ministry and mission."

Charles Hewlett, Former Principal of Carey Baptist College, Church Coach, Greenlane Christian Centre. Author of *Hurting Hope: what parents feel when their children suffer.*

"Daphne Marsden contributes a timely voice to this very important conversation. Her treatment of the complex topic of intimate partner violence in the context of the church's response is evocative, well-researched and compassionate. It is my hope that many pastors, counsellors and lay people will read this book in order to change the story from victimizing or further traumatising the victims.

This book is in line with the tender heart of Jesus who is characterised in Isaiah with these words: "A bruised reed he will not break... In faithfulness he will bring forth justice". It is a call for pastors or any Christian who encounters a woman caught in the life-and-death (in every sense of those words) situation of domestic violence, to offer a personal extension of the redemptive work of God in the world, empowering her with healthy theology rather than adding to her feelings of being trapped or displeasing God by leaving a context of abuse.

The burden of this book is about empowerment and justice for the oppressed, passionately debunking myths around forgiveness that have not been helpful for this vulnerable population. Issues like reconciliation, forgiveness, and healing flow out of the character of God's way of being with the world, which is anything but violent or abusive.

This book has power to change the course of a listening church to realign with the Triune God's agenda of shalom for everyone, even the perpetrator, who is deeply lost and reacting from a place of fear not love."

Dr Ruth A. Lawson-McConnell, Counsellor, Supervisor, Trainer, MNZAC, NZCCA (Affiliate), Clinical Neuropsychotherapy Practitioner (IACN trainee), Partners of Sex Addicts Trauma Specialist (APSATS trainer)

"In *Dishonoured and Unheard: Christian Women and Domestic Violence*, author Daphne Marsden explains the dilemma of and unpacks the primary obstacles faced by Christian victims of domestic violence in the church today. In the words of survivors and experts alike, she puts a face on the 1 in 3 women who so often suffer silently in their pews, and as well as those who speak up only to be disbelieved, blamed or even punished for doing so.

Drawing on her own research, as well of many others, including renowned experts and pioneers in addressing violence against women and religion, Rev Dr Marie M. Fortune, biblical scholar Catherine Clark Kroeger, and sociologist Nancy Nason-Clark, Marsden digs deep into the thorny theological issues of divorce, wifely submission, male entitlement, a husband's headship, and the meaning of forgiveness. She challenges the common biblical misinterpretations and misrepresentations that are so often used to support, justify, or sanction abuse within Christian families. By explaining the scriptural principles and ideals for a loving partnership based on mutuality, she offers a picture of Christian marriage as it was intended to be, a blessing to husbands and wives rooted in equality, respect and mutual submission to each other out of reverence for Christ.

There is something in this book for everyone interested in domestic violence and the church. Victims and survivors reading *Dishonoured and Unheard* will find validation and support for moving forward with the assurance that God hates abuse and does not expect or require them to suffer or submit to abuse. Pastors and lay leaders will gain a new understanding of the grim realities of domestic violence in families of faith, and the importance of focusing on safety for victims and accountability for abusers. Domestic violence victim advocates will gain an appreciation of the power and influence of a victim's faith walk, and new insights into its potential to encourage and support her in pursuing a life free of violence."

Julie Owens, Domestic Violence Expert Consultant, U.S. Department of Justice Office for Victims of Crime Training and Technical Assistance Centre. Domestic violence survivor; victim advocate; member Presbyterian Church-USA.

"This carefully written, compact, book offers the average pastor or layperson the ability to understand the dynamics of abuse within households of faith and to see, in particular, how the concept of forgiveness impacts battered Christian women everywhere. Interweaving the stories of abused women with the words and comfort of Scripture, Daphne Marsden has written from her heart, and from her studies, and every pastor needs to hear what she has to say."

Nancy Nason-Clark, Professor of Sociology University of New Brunswick Canada. Author of many books, including *The Battered Wife. How Christians Confront Family Violence, No Place for Abuse: Biblical & Practical Resources to Counteract Domestic Violence* (written with Catherine Clark Kroeger), and *Religion and Intimate Partner Violence: Understanding the Challenges and Proposing Solutions.*

"This concise and easy to read small book will be an invaluable resource to any pastor or Christian leader working alongside families, but also offers well researched insights that will illuminate the issues for the person struggling within an abusive marriage. Saturated with scripture and insights from experts in this field,

Daphne has brought together the wisdom around forgiveness, covenant, divorce and male headship. Every mature Christian needs an understanding of these issues to better operate and give wisdom in the context of human relationships. Read this, it could change your life!"

Ruby Duncan, Neighbourhood & Justice Initiatives Team Leader Baptist Churches of New Zealand.

Contents

Acknowledgements

The result that is this little book is due to the generous giving of time, expertise and kindness from a supportive group of people. I am especially grateful to Judith McInnes and Alistair Mackenzie who patiently helped with advice, formatting and encouragement. Experts and my heroines: the late Dr Catherine Clark Kroeger, Dr Nancy Nason- Clark and Julie Owens have invested their lives into researching and advocacy for victims, and have provided me with inspiration. To the Trustees and my wonderful co-workers at Project Esther Trust, I am fortunate to have had your companioning as we got this done. Thank you also to loving friends and family who often asked, "How is the book coming along?"

Most significantly thank you to the women who shared their journeys and insights with the hope that their sharing would enable others who are on a similar path.

Introduction

Mary: The first time that Sam hit me—he just ... I was on the bed and he was slapping my face, side to side like that, you know (moves head) ... hurting ... and I thought to myself, "I'm not going to cry, I'm not going to let him see that this is upsetting me". And I just lay there and let him do it to me. Where did that come from?! I've not a clue. He just slapped, slap, slap (like this)... and I didn't know it was abuse. I just lay there, thinking, "There's one thing I'm not going to let him do to me—and that is I'm not going to let him break me" ... that was so early in our marriage, like, maybe a year into our marriage ... Something just shifted in my thinking towards him from then on and I was married to him for 13 years.

Covenant is something to be taken seriously. I didn't think God ever broke covenants—so if we made a covenant with God, then we shouldn't break it either. Which sort of takes my mind down the road to—well, how bad is divorce, then?

In a few sentences Mary invites us into her pain-ridden world as a Christian woman experiencing domestic abuse.

The world of a woman who is trying to navigate an abusive Christian marriage is burdensome. As well as her spiritual beliefs about marriage, there is relentless need for caution. Women talk of watching over their shoulder, wondering if (when) his mood will change, and trying to avoid conflict. Women struggle with propping up a sick relationship, living sacrificially and giving up their own entitlement to peace and safety, leaving to protect children, or choosing to stay for the sake of provision for children. There is the fear of shame and misunderstanding from relatives, workmates, and church friends if she leaves. People who matter to the woman might be shocked and judgemental. Others don't see the whole story of a relationship and make assumptions that all is well. If she leaves, she fears being seen to be compromising her faith beliefs about marriage. Christian family or friends may observe strain and make assumptions that whatever is wrong can be fixed with prayer, forgiveness, and commitment. There can be a lot to cover up. Huge effort is required to keep on hoping for change. Accommodating one's own behaviour to manage an abusive husband is a heavy burden.

Mary already had in her mind the message, "You made your bed, now lie in it." Her mother had told her that from a young age. Like others, Mary went to her church community. Instead of honouring her sacred vulnerability, she was offered another blanket of guilt, and reminded that her marriage was a covenant; and asked, did she want to please God? Was she willing to turn the other cheek? She wondered, do I have to do that literally? And how much is enough, or too much?

Mary's world of isolation, darkness, and secret suffering was layered with skewed theology and misuse of scripture; another blanket for her bed of suffering—a dark, damp, heavy, cold blanket. Mary needed a blanket that was gentle, maybe merino, or a soft down feather quilt which was light and protective. That is what she deserved. That's what Jesus, the lover of justice and compassion, would give her. The scriptures he would guide her towards would be quite different to the ones she had been encouraged to dwell on. Instead, her church dished out the standard grey heavy blanket of "try harder," and smothered her hope.

So where has my desire to write a book for Christian women enduring or recovering from domestic abuse come from? The answer can be summed up in two words: "frustration" and "injustice".

For many years I have been blessed to serve in the pastoral care area of a vibrant evangelical church. I would hear abused women sharing how they do not always get the help they need from their churches. Abuse also significantly featured in my own upbringing. Mary's comments were heard as part of my research for a Master of Theology thesis. I sought to explore the experiences Christian women face as they suffer abuse at the hands of their husbands and then, beyond this, as they seek help from their church communities.

I became convinced that a sounder basis for understanding and responding to domestic violence within the Christian home, from a biblical perspective as well as practically, needs to be identified and embraced. (In this book the terms "family violence", "domestic violence", and "intimate partner violence" will be used interchangeably, depending on the literary sources that are being referenced). Women like Mary have been misled theologically. This is unjust. Our sisters in Christ deserve sounder pastoral and biblical responses. It behoves us as faith communities to use scripture wisely; to build up, encourage, bring life, and to make new.

The primary quest of this small book is to focus on the use of scripture in the pain-filled places of domestic abuse. It is a pastoral attempt to offer empowering biblical perspectives to Christian women who are being abused and to encourage women who are in life-long recovery. It is also for those who walk alongside, who listen, counsel, or give advice; be they pastors, church ministry leaders, or friends. The material focuses on use of scripture and has been drawn from experts in the field with the intention that it be a helpful resource.

Of course there are other issues women face in the context of abuse, not the least being physical safety, or dealing with perpetrators and legal systems. The bibliography will provide options to explore these and other important aspects. An appendix at the end of the book lists the website where my original thesis can be found.

Generously and graciously women who have experienced abuse have allowed their precious stories to be used (anonymously). Aspects of their stories will be interspersed throughout. Fictional stories and phrases are also incorporated to illustrate principles.

It is my heartfelt prayer that, particularly as women read this material, God's arms of compassion and voice of justice would be experienced in new and life-giving ways.

Chapter One

My Neighbour

Many years ago I was stunned to see my neighbour's face misshapen and swollen with two black eyes. I had never seen two black eyes on a person. I assumed there must have been some kind of an accident, or perhaps a bad fall. She had small children and was pregnant. In my ignorance initially I couldn't fathom that her husband would do this to her. Though secretive and evasive about her injuries, she was asking for help. The experience cemented my stereotypical view about the nature of domestic violence. Her husband was an alcoholic, they were financially stretched, and the curtains of their house were often closed during the daytime. Even though the car was in the driveway no one answered the door when I would knock. Back then, I concluded her circumstances were the norm—that was how life was for women who are victims of domestic violence.

Since that experience, work and study has lead me into many more encounters with women who were living under the black cloud of abuse. The stereotypical view from the past was brought into question; I came to new realisations. Many women in different realms suffer the blight of domestic violence: wealthy women, pregnant women, women in prison, those successful in business, students, professional women, mothers, and grandmothers. Increasingly, women with whom I was acquainted sought me out and shared how abuse was a part of their story. I was often surprised as there had been no inkling and I had never suspected these friends, colleagues, extended family, close and distant acquaintances were victims of domestic abuse. Such is the nature and secrecy that surrounds the issue.

A range of scenarios follows.

Maria is a successful businesswoman in a senior position at a well-known manufacturing company. Her skills and abilities brought the company its high profile and profits. She leads a large staff team and navigates significant financial transactions. However, her husband's abusive behaviours were not observed by others. He

5

kept to himself financial decisions he made on her behalf. He was sulky, quiet, and seethed when he didn't want to do something Maria wanted, especially when it involved visiting family or participating in family events. He hit her, shouted at her, and deprived her of affection. At the time her sister died he was unkind and vindictive with his words and actions. It transpired that his non-transparent financial decisions have left Maria disadvantaged and responsible for debt. The demise of their relationship has come as a surprise to family and work colleagues. They never had reason to suspect Maria's private life was fraught. Maria hid the dark details of abuse from others. She thought if she just kept accommodating him she could manage. Her husband was wonderful much of the time, but better and stable times became less frequent.

Lizzie has an all too familiar story; her husband had an addiction to pornography. Her abhorrence and non-participation in his pursuit has led to her husband's neglect and disinterest in her. The bulk of his spare time was spent in the study. He prioritized his time at the computer over time with Lizzie and the children. Lizzie got frustrated about her husband's self-indulgent attitude with the family computer and their children being exposed to such material. She was especially disappointed and angered that her adolescent daughter was aware of the nature of her father's addiction and had come across pornographic material. There was the shame and abuse of sexual intimacy being impacted and influenced by her husband's pornographic worldview. All of this remained her secret.

Some men may smugly consider this kind of activity outside the realms of domestic abuse. However, like any addiction, it contributes dysfunction and secrecy to a trusting relationship. A wife's emotional wellbeing and confidence erodes enduring a husband's pornographic obsession. It is a humiliating and abusive experience for a wife. It is a misuse of trust and power, a form of unfaithfulness and desertion to neglect or abuse the right of a wife to honest, safe, and healthy sexual intimacy.

Katie, in her late teens, said her boyfriend was awful to her but only when he was drunk. At such times he was mean and called her names or criticised her friends and family. But she believed the gains in the relationship made the bad times bearable. "It's not that bad," she would say. "He will get better and I can help him." She was sure he would change with her help. He usually said sorry the day after he had hurt her. She expressed confidence in their future as he was so committed and very interested in her. She had apps on her phone so he knew where she was at any time and what she spent money on. Katie was disappointed he didn't want to meet in the company of her friends, or meet her parents. He only wanted to be with her at his flat where they could be on their own. Katie had not told her parents that her boyfriend physically hurt her.

She didn't comprehend that she was in an abusive relationship. Like others in her situation she was holding on to the dream that he would change with her influence. This hope for change was not going to happen with her input alone. There were signs of real dysfunction and potential for increasing control of her by her boyfriend. She was afraid of him and intimidated by him. She had lost her peace of mind. She excused and minimised his behaviours. He got explosively angry. He was isolating her from friends and family. She was secretive about the nature of their relationship. He was possessive and wanted to know her whereabouts.

If Katie were to leave this relationship behind, she needed to hear her own wisdom which was lurking in her feelings of fear, misgivings, discomfort, and the desire for change. Her idea of progress was to see him change. My idea of progress would see her leave this relationship or any like it. I wanted her to listen to the seeds of her own wisdom, to keep questioning the dynamics of the relationship, and not blindly resign herself to its cage. If he had hit her a few times he would assault her again.[1] While she assumed their future to be hopeful and rosy and contemplated a permanent relationship, half the men who abuse their wives also abuse their children,[2] and sexual assault occurs in approximately 45 percent of abusive relationships.[3]

---

[1] http://dhhs.ne.gov/children_family_services/Documents/2003silence.pdf

[2] Justin S. and Lindsey A. Holcomb, *Is It My Fault? Hope and Healing for those Suffering Domestic Violence* (Illinois, USA: Moody Publishers, 2014), 61, citing

Maddie is in her early thirties with two pre-schoolers. She assumed she would live happily ever after. She claims her great dilemma is that her husband of six years does not hit her. She believes if he did she would be justified to get out of the relationship. She endures daily verbal abuse and is called derogatory names, told she is stupid, and sworn at. Her husband tells Maddie that it is her behaviour that is to blame for his intolerance of her. She is told she is fat, lazy, and irresponsible, and doesn't deserve to be called a wife or decent mother. He has cut her off from visiting her mother and from her sister who also has small children. He doesn't want her family's influence rubbing off on his children. She is lonely and hides her social life which is limited. He checks her texts, email, and Facebook sites, making disapproving comments about people she relates to. She would like to enrol the older child into preschool and get part time work as her husband controls the finances and doesn't allow her to spend without his consent. He won't agree to her getting work. He believes her place is to be at home. Her statements include: "He never really hurts me", "It's not like he ever beats me", "If I tried harder maybe he would improve", "Others are worse off", "Children need two parents." Maddie is experiencing emotional abuse. She endures shouting, being called names, being blamed and shamed. "Isolation, intimidation, and controlling behaviour are also signs of emotional abuse".[4] Economic abuse is also her lot, which can include

---

Murray Straus, "Ordinary Violence, Child Abuse and Wife Beating: What Do They have in Common?" in *Physical Violence in American families*, ed. Murray Straus and Richard Gelles (New Brunswick, NJ: Transition, 1990), 403-24.

[3] Ibid., 74, citing J. C. Campbell and K. Soeken, "Forced Sex and Intimate Partner Violence: Effects on Women's Risk and Women's Health," *Violence Against Women* 5, 2 (July 1999): 1017–35; and Campbell et al, "Assessing Risk Factors for Intimate Partner Homicide," *NIJ Journal* 250 (2003): 14-19; R. Acierno, H. S. Resnick, and D. G. Kilpatrick, "Health Impact of Interpersonal Violence: Prevalence Rates, Case Identification, and Risk Factors for Sexual Assault, Physical Assault, and Domestic Violence in Men and Women," *Behavioural Medicine* 23 (1997): 53–64; J. P. Quillan, "Screening for Spousal or Partner Abuse in a Community Health Setting," *Journal of the American Anatomy of Nurse Practitioners* 8 (1996): 155–60.

"withholding money and basic necessities, restricting you to an allowance, sabotaging your job, and stealing from you or taking your money".[5]

These varied scenarios highlight how abuse remains hidden and not accounted for. Some women in these accounts did not consider that they were being abused or controlled; other women acknowledge there is abuse occurring and choose to remain in the relationship.

In the next chapter we will consider why, even with the recognition of abuse, some women choose to stay.

---

[4] Ibid., 37.

[5] Ibid.

Chapter Two

Why Stay? What is Family Violence, and How Bad is It?

When we read the previous scenarios or think of particular women we know who are dealing with similar circumstances we can't help wondering, "Why doesn't she just leave?" Clearly it is neither easy nor simple.

Experts tell us that the reasons are varied and complex. Christian sociologist and researcher Nancy Nason-Clark and theologian Catherine Clark Kroeger have written, worked together, and produced many books and resources jointly and separately. I will often draw on their comprehensive, helpful work as I go. They highlight some particular reasons women remain in abusive relationships—fear,[1] finances, and a fantasy of change.[2] Fear is a dominant factor. Women are afraid that previous threats will be carried out on them and their children. They assume that leaving will not equate to safety but will make things worse. Statistics show that leaving a relationship of abuse is indeed a most dangerous time for many women. Many domestically related homicides of women and children by abusive partners take place following the decision to flee.[3] Women tell of being afraid to leave abusive husbands who have previously threatened that a separation would result in the husband instigating a legal process to gain custody of their children.

Financial constraints and dependence push women to remain in abusive relationships.[4] There will be the harsh awareness of no, or reduced, financial support if she leaves the relationship. When

---

[1] Nancy Nason-Clark and Catherine Clark Kroeger, *No Place for Abuse: Biblical and Practical Resources to Counteract Domestic Violence* (Downers Grove, Illinois: Inter-Varsity Press, 2001), 34.

[2] Ibid., 35.

[3] Ron Clark, *Freeing the Oppressed: A Call To Christians Concerning Domestic Violence* (Eugene, Oregon: Cascade Books, 2009), 10.

[4] Nason-Clark and Kroeger, *No Place for Abuse*, 35.

there are joint debts and mortgages women often have limited capacity to financially provide for their children.

For many women the choice to remain is driven by the hope for change. A woman hopes the abusive behaviours might settle or cease.[5] Sometimes women believe they can influence these changes.[6]

Christian women also choose to stay in abusive relationships for some of these reasons. In addition, the way they understand their faith significantly influences their tolerance of abuse and reluctance to leave. Christian values, beliefs, and understanding of scripture complicate issues for a Christian woman having to navigate the presence of abuse.

While secular women may be encouraged to leave violent relationships, within the church leaving is a possibility that is frequently denied and discouraged for a Christian woman. Women seeking help from the church speak of being asked questions which relate to the Bible. Such questions can include:

Have you prayed for your husband?

Have you forgiven him?

What have *you* done that has contributed to the conflict?

Have you been submissive?

Didn't you promise to stay for better or worse in your wedding vows?

Doesn't the Bible say we are to suffer for our faith?

Each of these questions is undergirded by and justified with traditional understandings of particular scriptures, such as forgiving seventy times seven (Matthew 18:21–22), women remaining silent (1 Corinthians 14:34–35), and wives submitting to their husbands (Ephesians 5:22–24; Colossians 3:18).

---

5   Ibid.

6   Clark, *Freeing the Oppressed*, 22.

"Domestic violence"—what does it mean?

Christian writers Justin and Lindsey Holcomb have theological and practical expertise about Christian domestic violence. They give us a helpful definition:

> Domestic violence is a pattern of coercive, controlling, or abusive behavior that is used by one individual to gain or maintain power and control over another individual in the context of an intimate relationship. This includes any behaviors that frighten, intimidate, terrorize, exploit, manipulate, hurt, humiliate, blame, injure, or wound an intimate partner.[7]

Nancy Nason-Clark explains, "The consequences of family violence are far-reaching and enduring for its victims: in addition to physical and emotional pain, there is the violation of the trusting relationship which may never be resolved. For religious victims, their spiritual journey may be adversely affected as well."[8]

The nature and extent of domestic violence— how bad is it really?

Violence is a major cause of death and disability for women aged between 16 and 44.[9] Globally, the World Bank estimates that violence against women is as serious a cause of death and incapacity among women of reproductive age as cancer, and is a greater cause of ill health than traffic accidents and malaria combined. In a majority of cases, the abuser will be a member of the woman's own family or someone known to her.[10] The most

---

[7]   Holcomb, *Is It My Fault?*, 57.

[8]   Nancy Nason-Clark, *The Battered Wife: How Christians Confront Family Violence* (Louisville, Kentucky: Westminster John Knox Press, 1997), 3.

[9]   UNIFEM, "Not a Minute More: Ending Violence Against Women," (New York: United Nations Development Fund for Women, 2003), 8. These statistics incorporated countries within Europe, the United Kingdom, and the United States of America. Violence against women in third world countries could only be referred to in general terms.

[10] Ibid., citing the World Health Organization *World Report on Violence and Health*, Geneva, Switzerland, World Health Organization; and Heise, Ellsberg and Gottemoeller, *Ending Violence Against Women*, Population Reports, Series L,

common form of violence experienced by women globally is intimate partner violence.[11]

New Zealand has its own domestic violence issues which are highlighted in the following statistics:

NZ Police recorded a family violence investigation on average every five and a half minutes in 2014. 76% of family violence incidents are NOT reported to Police.[12] 101,981 family violence investigations were recorded by NZ Police in 2014, up 7% from 95,101 in 2013.[13]

In 2010/11, 58% of all reported violent crime in New Zealand was family violence:

- 45% of abductions, kidnappings and threatening behaviour
- 75% of serious assaults
- 64% of all assaults
- 33% of sexual assaults.
- 84% of those arrested for family violence are men; 16% are women.[14]

Partner Abuse:

- 1 in 3 women experience physical or sexual violence from a partner in their lifetime.[15]
- an average of 12 women and 4 men a year were killed in the context of Intimate Partner Violence, (which includes the deaths of new [male] partners of women, by the woman's ex-partner).[16]

No. 11 (Baltimore: John Hopkins University School of Public Health, 1999).

[11] United Nations, *Ending Violence Against Women: From Words to Action*, ed. Secretary General (New York, USA: United Nations 2006), 111.

[12] http://areyouok.org.nz/family-violence/statistics/ as at 31/10/16.

[13] Ibid.

[14] http://www.areyouok.org.nz/files/statistics/ItsnotOK_recent_family_violence_stats.pdf (as at 11/07/14).

[15] http://areyouok.org.nz/family-violence/statistics/ as at 31/10/16.

[16] Ibid.

- 76 per cent of recorded assaults against females are committed by an offender that is identified as family.[17]
- Between 33 to 39% of New Zealand women experience physical or sexual violence from an intimate partner in their lifetime.[18]
- Women's Refuge received 81,990 crisis calls in 2014/15, and provided services to 16,507 women and children.[19]

The online news website stuff.co.nz reported in 2011 on results of research carried out by UN Women, and a local Ministry of Social Development survey:

The Government needs to immediately launch an inquiry into why New Zealand has such high domestic violence and maternal mortality rates compared with other Organisation for Economic Development and Co-operation (OECD) countries, the head of United Nations Women New Zealand says. A report by UN Women was released in Wellington today and canvassed 22 developed nations about subjects including domestic violence and maternal mortality. New Zealand was ranked either at or near the bottom of the countries in the study in both areas and UN Women New Zealand national president Rae Julian called on the Government to "actively investigate the causes of New Zealand's high level of maternal mortality and issues of partner violence against women". Initiatives needed to be implemented to address the issues highlighted by the report, she said. The study found a third of the country's women had reported experiencing physical violence from a partner during the period 2000 to 2010. That puts New Zealand as the worst affected of the 14 countries which responded to the question. In the past year, New Zealand rated 11th out of the 12 countries that reported violence against women, with only Finland rating lower. Sexual violence from partners showed a similar trend, with New Zealand coming out worst of the 12 countries that responded to the question. The closest ranked to New Zealand's 14 per cent was Norway, at 9 per cent. In the past year, 2 per cent of women reported experiencing sexual violence from a partner, ranking bottom of the list.

The report follows a Ministry of Social Development study released last month which found more than a quarter of the country's children had witnessed family violence. The survey was published in the latest social policy journal and interviewed almost 2100 children nationwide, the Sunday News reported. Of those surveyed, 27 per cent had seen physical violence against an

---

[17] Ibid.

[18] https://womensrefuge.org.nz/wp-content/uploads/2015/11/Domestic-violence-statistics-NZ.pdf as at 31/10/16.

[19] Ibid.

adult and most of those incidents had been in the home. When adults children loved were involved in the violence it had more impact on the child and also affected how they coped, and their decisions about telling anyone, with most too scared to speak out, the report found.[20]

These statistics and reports reveal how very widespread domestic violence is in New Zealand, and the way it is impacting and affecting many families. To read that more than a quarter of our children are witnessing abuse is heart breaking. It seems as well the Christian community is not adequately aware that Christian families are not immune to domestic abuse. For many women a commitment to her faith and church community does not mean the absence of abuse.

Steven Tracy, a Phoenix seminary professor who specialises in sexual addiction, child abuse, and protection says, "The scope and consequences of domestic violence are often misunderstood and rarely addressed in the evangelical church."[21] He cites a 1998 US Justice Department analysis of crime which showed that more than 40 percent of adult female hospital emergency room visits are caused by male intimate partners. The same article references a study that focused on 1,000 battered women. Sixty-seven percent of the women in the study said they attended church; one third of these women sought help. Of these, fully two-thirds said their church leaders were not helpful in addressing their situation.[22]

Nancy Nason-Clark and Catherine Clark Kroeger also highlight a number of related and alarming facts.[23] "The United States Surgeon General has reported that domestic violence accounts for more adult female emergency room visits than traffic accidents,

---

[20] http://www.stuff.co.nz/national/5332717/NZ-worst-for-domestic-violence-UN-report 24/07/2011.

[21] Steven R Tracy, "Patriarchy and Domestic Violence: Challenging Common Misconceptions," *Journal of the Evangelical Theological Society* 50 (2007): 573.

[22] Ibid.

[23] Nancy Nason-Clark and the late Catherine Clark Kroeger are major commentators in the area of domestic abuse within the Christian family. This is why their views have been given such prominence in this introductory chapter.

muggings, and rapes combined, and is the greatest single cause of injury to American women."[24] They also comment that around the world, "gender violence causes more death and disability among women aged 15–24 than cancer, malaria, traffic accidents or war."[25] Significantly "researchers in the field of family violence have consistently argued that the rate of male violence against women knows no religious boundaries."[26] "The family may be sacred, but sometimes it is not safe."[27] There are many women and children who leave church on Sunday and return home to abuse.[28]

Research reveals the prevalence of family violence in religious homes is as common as in the wider community,[29] also many religious victims do not disclose their abuse.[30] Christian women and their church communities may be tolerating violence and limiting victims' options for a solution due to ignorance, theological influences, and traditional mindsets. Very often the suggested solution for abuse issues draws on the Bible and particular interpretations of some scriptures. These interpretations can be unhelpful. Another renowned expert we will draw on is

---

[24] Catherine Clark Kroeger and Nancy Nason-Clark, *Refuge from Abuse: Healing and Hope for Abused Christian Women* (Downers Grove: Inter-Varsity Press 2004), 39, citing Evan Stark and Anne Flitcraft, "Medical Therapy as Repression: The Case of Battered Women," *Health and Medicine* (Summer/Fall 1982): 32. The same statistical claim is made at http://www.strengthenoursisters.org/facts_ domestic_violence.html, referring to Stark and Flitcraft's research "Violence Among Intimates: An Epidemiological Review," in *Handbook of Family Violence*, ed. Haslett et al (New York: Springer, 1987), 293-317.

[25] Ibid., 39, citing *News from the World Association of Christian Communication* 204, March 1998.

[26] Nason-Clark, *The Battered Wife: How Christians Confront Family Violence*, 59, citing L. Freedman, "Wife Assault," in *No Safe Place: Violence Against Women and Children*, ed. C Guberman and M Wolfe (Toronto: Women's Press, 1985): 41–60.

[27] Ibid., 1.

[28] Nason-Clark and Kroeger, *No Place for Abuse*, 44.

[29] Ibid., 20.

[30] Ibid.

Marie Fortune, founder of the Center for the Prevention of Sexual and Domestic Violence, now known as Faith Trust Institute. Fortune highlights how both victims and abusers misuse scripture and theology to justify family violence.

> This misuse has resulted from a lack of understanding of the nature and causes of violence and from a failure to recognise how dangerous - even lethal - it can be. This misuse has also resulted from a misappropriation of religious teaching. The silence that the religious community has maintained on the subject has contributed to the lack of understanding by failing to correct it.[31]

Christian women in abusive relationships experience the same physical, emotional and financial fears as other women, and the same hopes for change in their husbands. But they are also more inclined to remain in abusive relationships because of spiritual beliefs, which they have been told are solidly grounded in scripture.

In the following chapters we want to examine some of these beliefs more closely by exploring typical pastoral conversations related to the issues of forgiveness, marriage as a covenant, and the concepts of headship and submission.

---

[31] Marie M Fortune, *Violence in the Family: A Workshop Curriculum For Clergy And Other Helpers* (Cleveland, Ohio: Pilgrim Press, 1991), 5.

Chapter Three

Pastoral Conversations Regarding Forgiveness

Linda: I think Brent knows it's wrong to hit me as he always says sorry afterwards. But when I say, "You're always saying sorry," he just says back, "I said sorry didn't I? What more do you want?" He brings up the Bible and verses about forgiving and turning the other cheek and God forgetting our sin. He says that if I wanted to be a true Christian wife I should apply those truths otherwise I am just being judgemental and seeing the speck in my brother's eye and not the log in my own.

I feel I have to forgive him because the Bible does say those things. At the same time I know I will be hurt again and Brent will be saying the same things again. Is this what God wants from me? Doesn't God care that I get hurt, I feel afraid? So much of my energy goes into reading Brent's moods to see if I can lessen the tension. Sometimes as soon as he walks in after work, I can tell if he is in a mood and I send the kids to their rooms so they're not around.

I've always thought if I kept on forgiving Brent he would change, that my tolerance and patience would be a good witness. You know, like that verse that says a quiet word turns away wrath, but nothing seems to change. I feel like a bad wife, and a bad mother too as I am afraid a lot of the time and I can't hide everything from the kids. One of my boys gives me a cuddle sometimes and I think he wants to comfort me even though I try to not let anything show.

I don't know what all the promises about protection mean in the Bible. God doesn't seem to protect me or the kids and then I have to turn around and say its ok, it's behind us, but it's not ok, it's going to happen again. Is it because I am holding a grudge that Brent keeps hurting me?

When I hear Linda's anguish I imagine a vortex where one goes round and round trying to do the right thing and getting nowhere. While trying to climb higher she sinks down further and further into the wearying darkness. I feel disappointed that Linda doesn't comprehend the righteous anger God has towards her plight. Linda does not know that God is on her side, the side of the oppressed. I can't help but wonder what has been going on in our church communities, when women like Linda don't experience Christians modelling God's intent to shield the vulnerable from wickedness. God's high priorities of justice and safety are being diluted by

19

human mindsets that place less value on these principles. These pressures to mindlessly forgive are a form of the wolf in sheep's clothing. She is being guilelessly devoured.

Challenges involved in forgiveness

When it comes to abuse and forgiveness there are significant challenges to be faced on all sides: for victims, perpetrators, and those on the side-lines.

Linda knows that she has complex issues to process. She feels she has to forgive, as the Bible requires. But from personal experience her offer of forgiveness will not stop her encountering more abuse. How does Linda reconcile not wanting to forgive when she knows that God commands that we forgive each other? This is not a subject that has easy answers.

When I talk with women like Linda about forgiveness, knowing that abuse is still happening, I need to have carefully considered the issue beforehand. From my point of view, pastorally I have found it important that when a woman points to particular scriptures about forgiveness to use the opportunity to invite consideration about the context of those commonly quoted verses about forgiveness. To ask, whether the black and white assumptions, for instance, about needing to forgive seventy times seven, are what is actually intended? Sometimes abuse victims are not guided wisely in how to apply scriptures about forgiveness to their personal situation.

Certainly for women like Linda, who are still in an existing abusive relationship, forgiveness is not a black and white issue. Sadly, it has been their experience that well-meaning pastors or others in the Christian community encourage the victim to start on the path of forgiveness (with reconciliation almost a non-negotiable requirement), without enough thought as to whether that is honestly the first action that Jesus would have taken in the same situation. "One of the most common complaints of battered women is that they have been pressured into forgiving and 'turning the other cheek.'"[1]

Bible verses on forgiveness have often been poorly explained so that in turn they are applied incorrectly by a woman trying to make spiritual sense of the misery that she is suffering. I have seen that for Christian women in relationships where abuse is taking place, biblical misunderstandings of forgiveness can keep them bound and committed to relationships, even tolerating abusive behaviour. Such beliefs as "I must forgive him or God won't forgive me," or "I must forgive seventy times seven," are used by women like Linda as they consider their perceived obligations regarding forgiveness.

A big motivation for a victim to offer forgiveness repeatedly to an abusive husband is the scripture which implies how our own personal forgiveness by God is dependent on our forgiving others. Some scriptures tell us to forgive and make no mention of the requirement of a guilty partner to repent or say sorry. To complicate matters further there are several scriptures which highlight the requirement of a guilty person to repent.

I have found some very helpful theologians and Christian writers who care deeply about victims of abuse. In this and following chapters their insights about scripture and forgiveness offer fresh hope and options for women caught up in the complex circumstances of domestic abuse.

We consider in this chapter the challenges for victims in the absence of repentance, expectations of reconciliation, perpetrators and true justice, and giving advice using scripture.

Challenges for victims

Marie Fortune says forgiveness before justice represents cheap grace and helps neither victim nor offender. Instead it can be dangerous to the victim and suppress the possibility of reform for the abuser, effectively perpetuating the cycle of abuse in a relationship.[2] To simply say one is sorry or to offer an apology,

---

[1]   Pamela Cooper-White, *The Cry of Tamar: Violence Against Women And The Church's Response* (Minneapolis, Minnesota: Fortress Press, 1995), 252.

does not meet the standard of biblical repentance; there must be an accompanying change in behaviour.[3]

Nancy Nason-Clark and Catherine Clark Kroger share this perspective: "Forgiveness does not mean going on as though nothing ever happened. Neither God nor human beings can forgive in a vacuum. Repentance calls for a transformed attitude and lifestyle."[4]

Christian women living in abusive situations are often directed to apply scripture. They hope the offered forgiveness will bring healing, deal to emotional pain, and address complicated issues related to abuse. These hopes that abused women have regarding the benefits of forgiveness do not always lead to freedom, closure, or beneficial results. This in turn can lead to a greater sense of guilt and frustration and sometimes increased danger.

Experts inform us, and some of us know first-hand, that the experience of violent abuse tends to follow a predictable cycle. The first stage of abuse is the escalation of conflict; the second stage is the specific violence; this is followed by a third stage of contrition and requests for forgiveness.[5] Those victimised are most vulnerable at the third stage when a partner has expressed remorse and made promises to change, particularly if they subscribe to religious beliefs that urge them to forgive.[6] Such beliefs can prevent a woman from seeking physical safety.

Renowned theologian and writer Lewis Smedes contributes greatly to the discussion of these important issues. He says, "We don't have to tolerate what people do just because we forgive them

---

[2] Fortune and Adams, *Violence Against Women and Children*, 202.

[3] Craig Blomberg, "On Building and Breaking Barriers: Forgiveness, Salvation and Christian Counseling with Special Reference to Matthew 18:15-35," *Journal of Psychology and Christianity* 25, 2 (2006): 145.

[4] Nason-Clark and Kroeger, *No Place for Abuse*, 116–17.

[5] Carol L Schnabl Schweitzer, "Violence Against Women and Children: How Churches Can Respond," *Word and World* 24 (2004): 69.

[6] Ibid.

for doing it, forgiveness heals us personally. To tolerate everything only hurts us all in the long run."[7]

Kiera comments on her experience this way:

> We have to forgive people, but we also have to set boundaries very clearly. That's part of the forgiveness. That's part of the journey of them coming to forgiveness themselves. Well, actually I had to learn the hard way because that's an area I am very weak—because I let the perpetrator come right into private areas.
>
> And there the law helped me—protection orders were put into place, trespass orders were put into place—so there were boundaries that he was not to come close to here, and he had to stay away when we meet in public. But these boundaries—they were so important and necessary, and from those boundaries I actually learned to make boundaries. Like sometimes he would come to the door—even now he does it—he comes to the door, he throws something at me, and I've learned to say, "I'm sorry, I'm quite busy, I have to go soon and I'm closing the door now," and then I close the door. I could not do that as a newly separated person, I was too vulnerable.
>
> You learn with the years. He still comes and behaves badly, not too badly any more, but he is still on a journey to actually acknowledge the truth.

Carolyn Holderread Heggen is a therapist and writer in the area of abuse. She believes that simplistic, quick forgiveness that does not demand accountability and responsibility increases the possibility of ongoing violence.[8] She says that Lenore Walker's work tells us that women with strong religious backgrounds are often the least likely to believe that violence against them is wrong.[9] Marie Fortune suggests that in the violence cycle, the crisis phase (stage two) is often followed by remorse and loving behaviour and pleas for forgiveness (stage three). Complying with this pattern may simply extend or reinforce the abusive behaviour.[10]

---

[7] Lewis Smedes, *Forgive and Forget: Healing the Hurts We Don't Deserve* (New York: Harper Collins, 1984), 49.

[8] Carolyn Holderread Heggen, "Religious Beliefs and Abuse," in *Women, Abuse, and the Bible: How Scripture can be Used to Hurt or Heal,* ed. Catherine Clark Kroeger & James R Beck (Grand Rapids, Michigan: Baker Books, 1996), 27.

[9] Ibid., 18.

[10] Fortune and Adams, *Violence Against Women and Children,* 202.

Author and professor of New Testament, Craig Blomberg, says, "When there is not true repentance on the part of the abuser it can be counterproductive or even harmful to forgive."[11] He refers to Paul's recommendation that someone who is unrepentant and continuing to engage in sin should be held at arm's length from the church community. He also highlights God's judgement and consequences for the cruelty imposed by the unforgiving servant of Matthew 18:21–35.

So all these experts are telling us how offering forgiveness to an abuser needs careful consideration.

Forgiveness is not about tolerating ongoing abuse. Needs for ongoing safety may be jeopardised by an abuser who thinks all is fine, it's "business as usual" after a simple apology.

Does forgiveness mean I must reconcile?

The pressure for an abuse victim to forgive a perpetrator often includes expectations of reconciliation. This reflects a distorted belief that reconciliation is a pinnacle to which Christians who are estranged from each other should aspire.

In the helpful book by Catherine Clark Kroeger and Nancy Nason-Clark, *No Place for Abuse: Biblical and Practical Resources to Counteract Domestic Violence,* we read that the Bible does not insist on returning to a relationship where there has been conflict, violent or otherwise. In this regard we can look at the relationships between Paul and Barnabas, Peter and Paul, and Jacob and Esau. Even Joseph tested the genuineness of the repentance of his brothers.[12]

Melissa Miller, author and pastor, also draws on Joseph's story and points out that his willingness to forgive was dependent on a change in his brothers' behaviour.[13] However, the process was long and the outcome was dependent on his eldest brother Judah taking

---

[11] Blomberg, "On Building and Breaking Barriers," 146.

[12] Nason-Clark and Kroeger, *No Place for Abuse,* 116.

[13] Melissa A Millar, *Family Violence: The Compassionate Church Responds* (Waterloo, Ontario: Herald Press, 1994), 155.

full responsibility for past misdemeanours. She explains forgiveness as "letting go of resentment."[14] The Greek interpretation of forgive is "to leave" (*aphiēmi*). This relates to one's inner response of being gradually able to think of offences without "being overwhelmed by churning emotions of fear and rage."[15] While forgiveness means a survivor can let go of resentment, it does not necessarily mean that the relationship is reconcilable.[16] The Bible exhorts us to forgive others. It does not, however, insist that we return to the circumstances in which the offence(s) took place.[17] Forgiveness does not always involve reconciliation.

Catherine Clark Kroeger describes it like this:

> *Aphiemi*, the Greek word for "forgive" means "to put something away, set it free, as well to put one thing aside in order to move onto something else". Forgiveness is essentially a putting away of our anger toward another, putting it aside so that it no longer controls our lives. Only by doing so can we be free to move onto something better. We are told to "leave room for Gods wrath" (Romans 12:19 NIV), just as we are exhorted to be angry but not to sin (Ephesians 4:26; cf. Psalms 4:4; James 1:19-20). Apolyo, another word for forgiving, has as well the idea of loosing or freeing ourselves from anger and resentment toward another.[18]

Craig Blomberg draws on a helpful distinction made by psychologist John Berecz who describes two types of forgiveness. The first type involves fully fledged reconciliation.[19] It is dependent on cooperation between both parties.[20] The second type of forgiveness involves a release, where the parties separate. In a situation where there is abuse or adultery and a perpetrator is in denial of any wrongdoing, the victim may need to separate, making that decision by herself. If, however, there is an amicable divorce where "both parties agree repentance is not sufficient to salvage a

---

[14] Ibid., 153.

[15] Ibid., 154.

[16] Ibid., 153.

[17] Nason-Clark and Kroeger, *No Place for Abuse*, 113.

[18] Ibid., 115.

[19] Blomberg, "On Building and Breaking Barriers," 146.

[20] Ibid., 151.

marriage from the sins committed", one may speak of mutual forgiveness.[21] He says all of these types of forgiveness by the victim can be faithful to scripture and "may be the best that can be managed in this fallen world."[22]

Marie Fortune advocates a culture of repentance and forgiveness which can leave the door open for the option of reconciliation but the prospect of reconciliation must be approached with great care:[23]

> Reconciliation therefore means that the survivor and abuser no longer relate to each other as victim and abuser. The survivor is not powerless; the abuser is not overpowering and coercive. The survivor need not be fearful. Battering is no longer an option for the former abuser as he relates to the survivor. In this context, the survivor and former abuser may choose to renew an intimate relationship. Many formerly battered women desire to renew an intimate relationship. For them, reconciliation takes this specific form. Others never want to be in an intimate relationship with their former abuser again; for them reconciliation may mean clearly ending that relationship while being assured that their former abuser will not continue to pursue and harass them. [24]

Theologian and writer about forgiveness Lewis Smedes says that forgiveness is the key to wholeness for a victim, even for serious offences. Repentance must be part of the deal for reconciliation to take place but this is not always wise, possible, or necessary for a certain level or kind of forgiveness to be achieved. "We need to forgive the unrepentant for our own sake. We need to forgive people who do not care if only so that we do not drown in our own misery."[25] An individual can take ownership and responsibility to release forgiveness and although complete resolution, reconciliation, or even healing may not be achieved, nevertheless there is much freedom and healing to be achieved in applying biblical principles of forgiveness and by doing what is

---

[21]   Ibid., 146.

[22]   Ibid.

[23]   Fortune, *Violence in the Family: A Workshop Curriculum For Clergy And Other Helpers*, 185.

[24]   Ibid., 186.

[25]   Lewis Smedes, *Forgive and Forget*, 69.

possible. While the climax of forgiveness takes two, the reality of forgiveness can still be achieved without such a climax. You do not always need a thing whole to enjoy it at all.[26]

He rejects the view that forgiveness cannot happen unless people come together in a renewed, close and connected, mutually accepting manner, saying that even if people are not brought together in renewed relationship, expressed forgiveness can be experienced partially by a victim. "We need not deny ourselves the healing of incomplete forgiving: we can forgive and be free in our own memories."[27]

In relation to forgiveness and reconciliation, the preceding paragraphs have presented a range of views, understandings, and expectations held by the Christian community based on particular understandings of scripture. These views have found their way to varying degrees into the mindset and hearts of women living in the context of domestic violence or who have left an abusive or violent relationship. How appropriate some of these views are regarding reconciliation in the context of existing violence, as opposed to the forgiveness processes post-violence, are questions that are both challenging and complex.

An area of conflicted understanding relates to what forgiveness does or does not mean. Marie Fortune says that for a victim, "forgiveness is letting go of the immediacy of the trauma, the memory of which continues to terrorise the victim and limit possibilities."[28] She claims that memory is the lens through which we view the world and claims that when one forgives, the lenses are put aside but kept close at hand.[29] Melissa Millar asserts that "healing depends on remembering"[30] but that forgiveness and reconciliation are completely different.[31]

---

[26]   Ibid., 70.

[27]   Ibid.

[28]   Fortune, *Violence Against Women and Children: A Christian Theological Sourcebook*, 203.

[29]   Ibid.

[30]   Millar, *Family Violence: The Compassionate Church Responds*, 157.

Marie Fortune reinforces the point that forgiveness is not a starting point; it requires time and must be driven by the timetable of the victim. Forgiveness is part of healing, but that forgiveness does not mean forgetting. Trying to forget is a waste of valuable energy and "putting the memory into perspective so that it no longer dominates one's life is more useful."[32] Thus, she claims forgiveness does not need to mean trusting or returning to a relationship, and the choice to forgive ought not to be tied to decisions to reconcile.[33]

Lewis Smedes puts it tenderly when he says, "If they cannot or will not pay their fare [meaning take responsibility for wrongdoing] you will have to settle for your own healing, your private freedom from hate, and your own inner peace."[34]

Challenges for the perpetrator

For true justice to occur, forgiveness is conditional. Marie Fortune highlights three steps. The first step involves the perpetrator acknowledging responsibility for harm. The second step is the perpetrator's repentance with an emphasis on the need for fundamental change. The third step is restitution which acknowledges cost and includes an attempt to make right that which was broken.[35] While each of these steps is necessary for the offender, Fortune nevertheless acknowledges that often the offender is "unwilling or unavailable" to take them.[36]

As stated previously, Craig Blomberg advocates the need for repentance and claims that in Matthew 18:15–35, when a fellow

---

[31] Ibid., 153.

[32] Fortune and Adams, *Violence Against Women and Children: A Christian Theological Sourcebook*, 204.

[33] Ibid.

[34] Smedes, *Forgive and Forget*, 32.

[35] Fortune, *Violence Against Women and Children: A Christian Theological Sourcebook*, 202.

[36] Ibid.

Christian fails to repent, the appropriate response as prescribed in verse 17b is distancing from fellowship.[37] He says, however, that the disciplining of a fellow believer in the New Testament was "always restorative" and not "retributive in intent."[38] The well-being of all parties is dependent on change and "relationships clearly cannot move forward with 'business as usual' until the disputes that initiated the process of discipline are adequately resolved."[39]

He goes on to say that forgiveness cannot lead to reconciliation if one party is not willing to repent. Jesus' understanding of unlimited forgiveness as described in verse 22 means returning to the way things were prior to the offence.[40] In a battered wife scenario this often means offences, plural. Simply apologising does not "in and of itself constitute biblical repentance unless it is accompanied by a change in action."[41] Like Marie Fortune, he claims that in the absence of genuine repentance, it can be counterproductive and harmful to forgive within the framework of behaving as if all is well again. This stance means the offender "has no incentive to repent" and his sinful behaviour is reinforced.[42]

Megan didn't experience repentance:

> So I was able to forgive him for the affair, but I couldn't forgive him for the porn and for following up with these women, or texting them. He thought he was hiding it, but it was really, really obvious! He thought he was being pretty sneaky and smart and all the rest of it but the wife always knows. There were lots of examples but I had enough to know what was going on, and to know it was going on really, really regularly over the years. He wanted to stay married, but at the same time he had at this stage a real addiction to women on the internet—many who I think he connected up with, in one form or another—and I began to feel very uneasy that he was sleeping with other women. I

---

[37] Blomberg, "On Building and Breaking Barriers," 139.

[38] Ibid., citing C. F. D. Moule, *Forgiveness and Reconciliation: Biblical and Theological Essays* (London: SPCK, 1998).

[39] Ibid.

[40] Ibid., 140.

[41] Ibid., 145.

[42] Ibid., 146.

moved out of our bedroom, because I couldn't trust him to have safe sex with other people. It's very abusive to have your husband on the internet with other women.

I feel in some ways that he's got away with it—he's done all these awful things, but because there's not been a great big, out and out fight and screaming match and other things, that he's ... oh well...

In Matthew 3:8, Luke 3:8, Luke 17:3, Luke 19:8-9, Acts 26:20, and Ephesians 4:28, John the Baptist, Jesus, and Paul called for a high regard for repentant behaviour and attitude. Repentance is much more than an insincere utterance of "I am sorry." Repentance calls for a transformed attitude and lifestyle.[43] Such high expectations about repentance call into question suggestions that a woman who is a victim of ongoing abuse should forgive "seventy times seven."

Challenges for those on the side-lines

Christians believe that God's word is relevant to how we live our lives. Those using scripture in pastoral care need to be mindful of the original contexts in which these verses were communicated. These commonly used scriptures can be misused or misapplied.

For women functioning within a present and existing abusive relationship, forgiveness is not straightforward. God does not expect battered women to remain in a partnership where there is ongoing violence. Yet in some church communities this is the expectation and advice given. There are those who perceive staying as "bearing their cross", and that this is a true marker that one has successfully forgiven. However, putting up with abuse is not forgiveness.

To a victim living with violence, forgiveness towards their partner is offered for a variety of reasons—from confusion and wanting the (sometimes biblically misconstrued) spiritual benefits of one's own forgiveness, to the need to stay within the approval of Christian community, or even to de-escalate conflict.

---

[43] Nason-Clark and Kroeger, *No Place for Abuse*, 117.

Steven Tracy is cautious with the stance that if we don't forgive others we will not be forgiven ourselves. He challenges claims that forgiveness involves the restoration of trust, letting go of all emotions including fear, anger, suspicion, alienation, and mistrust.[44] This is an enormous step for an abused woman to take, and one that makes her vulnerable in a whole new way. When pastors are dealing with women who have asked for help in relation to domestic violence, they need to be aware of their vulnerability. He says that rather than encourage them towards a premature release of healthy emotions, there is good reason for abuse victims to hold on to mistrust and their fear of unrepentant abusers.[45] Mistrust and fear are often justified by experience and can enable choices by victims to remain safe or protective of themselves and others. Tracy promotes a style of forgiveness that pastors could do well to follow, which involves letting go of personal attempts for revenge and, where possible and appropriate, extending grace and kindness, not hatred. This offers hope for abuse survivors and provides a call to repentance for abusers.[46]

Based on her experiences, Ethel highlights this need to remember and thus remain safe:

> I have found forgiveness, although I still would like to understand more. I certainly think that "forgive and forget" is very dangerous. And forgiveness was one of the things I was trying focus on, to re-establish some kind of relationship with the man I had been married to ... because I was trying to be open and honest, and he was still the father of our daughter.

> I went to the minister and this time, instead of sending me back into the marriage (which is what he had done before), this time he said, "Look after your sacred self, and remember the pain of the past. Don't forget it. Remember the pain from when you were in that relationship, so that you don't go back into the same things that you have gotten out of. You have to remember, not forget."

---

44   Steven R. Tracy, "Sexual Abuse and Forgiveness," *Journal of Psychology and Theology* 27, 3 (1999): 220., citing David Augsburger in his two volume work, *Caring Enough to Forgive: True Forgiveness*, and *Caring Enough to Forgive: False Forgiveness* (Ventura, California: Regal Books, 1981).

45   Ibid.

46   Ibid., 227.

So I think forgiveness is about some honest recognition. And it's about grace, and realising it's not for me to judge and say somebody is evil if they do this or that or the other thing. There's grace in this, there is a bigger forgiveness, and forgiveness on my part—somehow there has to be for myself that kind of grace.

But also, it doesn't mean that I forget everything, and it also means that I focus on the actions that are harmful and injurious, rather than saying the person is wicked and evil. What they have done has been deeply injurious.

This idea of remembering, and thus remaining safe, resonates well with Lewis Smedes' earlier suggestion that forgiveness is essential for wholeness. He refers to the role of memory and processing thoughts in light of the bigger picture of understanding the complexity of sin and our common need of grace. He says "You will know that forgiveness has begun when you recall those who hurt you and feel the power to wish them well."[47] This statement can be of help to a woman processing historical abuse rather than in the context of existing abuse. It is hard to see how either Jesus or Paul expected a woman suffering repeated abuse to constantly forgive "seventy times seven," or to reconcile continuously in the absence of true repentance on the part of the perpetrator. Those giving pastoral advice need to acknowledge this difference and ask, "What would Jesus do?" He certainly wouldn't insist she returns to more abuse.

Steven Tracy helps us understand this when he explains, "While scripture does describe forgiveness as the removal or letting go of a debt (Matthew 6:12), forgiveness does not remove negative consequences for the one forgiven. Nor does it automatically grant trust and reconciliation."[48] He encourages a broad-range look at scripture to ascertain pertinent principles.[49]

---

[47] Smedes, *Forgive and Forget*, 29.

[48] Tracy, "Sexual Abuse and Forgiveness," 220, citing Doris Donnelly, "Forgiveness and Recidivism," *Pastoral Psychology*, 33 (1984): 15–24, and Andy Bustanoby, "How do you Forgive the Unrepentant?" *Leadership* 12 (1991): 98–104.

[49] Tracy, "Sexual Abuse and Forgiveness," 220.

Returning to Matthew 18:15–22, Craig Blomberg considers the immediate context within the chapter. He claims that the practice of forgiveness influences the wellbeing of a follower of Jesus in this life and the next. In these terms, forgiveness is not only possible but beneficial for individuals and for the community of faith. However, he goes to great lengths to stress the use of "brother or sister" in Matthew 18:15. This is to emphasise there was equality and no power imbalance between those addressed, since it was delivered solely to a select group of Jesus' followers.[50] Matthew 18:15–22 thus assumes forgiveness is expected within a context of equality as followers of Jesus.

So this cautioning advice occurs in the context of how Christians are to respond to fellow Christians who have sinned against them and includes aspects of humility, scandal, drifting from the faith, forgiveness, and discipline.[51] Jesus' instruction in this situation, as with other ethical directives, had less extreme offences in mind.[52] Exceptions here would include the situation of a constantly battered wife. Blomberg also believes it is misguided to apply verses 21–22 of Matthew 18 to addictive behaviours or abuse. To do so would merely encourage the continuation of hurtful patterns of behaviour when intervention could be redemptive.[53] A relationship where abuse is operating is not one of respectful, servant-oriented equality which Paul and Jesus advocated.

Christians ought to encourage perpetrators to take responsibility for their abusive behaviour, take steps to change, respect the boundaries of their victims and ensure there is no risk of a victim being further victimised.[54]

---

[50] Blomberg, "On Building and Breaking Barriers," 138.

[51] Ibid.

[52] Ibid.

[53] Ibid., 137.

[54] Tracy, "Sexual Abuse and Forgiveness," 224, citing J. G. Haber, *Forgiveness* (Savage, MD: Rowman and Littlefield, 1991), and Lewis Smedes, "Forgiving People Who Do Not Care," *Reformed Journal* 33 (1983): 13–18.

Conclusion

Women in abusive relationships carry heavy burdens of beliefs about forgiveness. Forgiveness is a gift that God intends to bring us all into freedom, but in circumstances relating to domestic violence it can be contaminated with false applications.

The dangers highlighted here are forgiving in the absence of changed behaviour, and issues relating to a high regard for reconciliation as an ideal goal.

Earlier in this chapter I noted that pastorally, I have to prepare with a thorough and correctly interpreted biblical understanding of these issues, before entering into a conversation. Pastorally it behoves us as ministers of the truth to use scripture ethically and responsibly to unburden and liberate. The story in Luke of the innocent woman who was bleeding has resonance. She too was ignorantly judged by others for her affliction. Jesus verbally countered biblical misconceptions about her status and then said in the hearing of all, "Woman be free...." If only.

Chapter Four

Divorce and the Permanence of Marriage

Amanda: I remember when I was younger Mum would always say, "Oh, you can't get divorced—when you marry, you marry for life." Mum's 78 now and maybe there are people who divorced or separated in her lifetime and they were always shunned. For me it was always "You make your bed, you lie in it." You've chosen, this is what you chose, and so you need to stay in it. There was Tamar in the Bible—she was raped. I guess that's kind of what I'm saying. Sometimes I felt like that in my marriage. Physically raped ... physically, things were torn away from me ... physically abused. Mentally and emotionally abused ... Discarded. I felt worthless, used, unworthy.

That's in my marriage, but also in the church ... I mean, "raped" is a really big word. But stripped, I suppose, would be better. When I left my husband, my so-called friends (I thought they were my friends and I thought they cared), they were kind of stripped away. They decided to move on. I saw the church marriage counsellor after I had left Jack. We'd spent so much time with her and she knew so much about me, and I just wanted to ... I just, I don't know ... I just wanted to talk to her and just explain, and it didn't happen—you know what I mean? I don't know how to put that. I often felt rejected. Blacklisted, or ... like a blemish, you know what I mean.

It's painful to listen to the dilemmas that affected Amanda. It reminds me of someone caught in a no-win situation. Whatever choice she makes brings doom. Being convinced God didn't want her to divorce, Amanda continued to live with abusive and dangerous behaviour. Decisions to remain or leave are not made lightly or painlessly. However, it seems that these decisions are often made with misguided understandings of particular scriptures. I feel frustrated that Amanda was never pointed to the variety of helpful references in the Bible about God, covenant, and divorce. Why do those with influence allow this to keep happening? God didn't put up with rubbish or bad behaviour from the Israelites! There were times when God said, "I have had enough. You've gone too far in your rebellion." "This disregard of my ways can't go on. You can't keep this up and expect me to prop up terrible behaviour and unfaithfulness." "No more help from me. You're on own. Sort yourselves out." Some scripture verses which describe such responses by God can be found in Isaiah 1:2-3,19-25; 3:1,14; Jeremiah 11:12; and 14:9.

Jesus' advocacy for women as victims in marriage gets left out too! And Paul said some really helpful things about marriage and mutuality. Both Paul and Jesus promoted marriage relationships operating with agreed mutuality rather than one person dominating another. There is so much more in the Bible than the arrogantly and ignorantly misused refrain "God hates divorce." There so much scripture which is helpful, empowering, and freeing.

What saddens me further is a woman's fear of judgement, criticism, and rejection from friends, family, and church if she is to leave her abusive husband. If only these were unnecessary concerns. She is (you are) worthy of even more support, encouragement, and compassion at such a time.

The dilemma regarding divorce

One of the biggest hurdles that an abused Christian woman (perhaps you) will face is the concept of marriage as a binding covenant, regardless of abuse. This chapter will again draw on theologians and writers who I have found offer helpful insights into commonly used scriptures. A sound but compassionate use of scriptures is an essential pastoral skill. This can enable abused women to process their choices with less guilt and fear.

Ron Clark is an author and pastor, with expertise in the area of domestic violence. He describes his perception of Christian women who are battered and how they experience church:

> They sit in the pews and see healthy families (or those that appear to be healthy) and feel guilty. They hear sermons critical of divorce and how Satan is causing the breakdown of the family. They hear how Jesus overcame evil by submission and endurance. They hear how marriage is not about happiness but commitment. They hear how we are victims of the wickedness of society, and that hope, prayer and endurance will bring us victory ...

> How has the faith community become an enabler of the abuse cycle? We hold to spiritual doctrines that further victimise victims and that keep abusers abusing. We turn our heads from the cries of the oppressed. We confront victims rather than abusers, and call for submission rather than justice.[1]

Carolyn Holderread Heggen says that while the Christian community needs to uphold the sacredness of marriage, they also need to understand the fair-minded nature of God in those instances where a marriage covenant has already been broken because of the existence of violence and abuse. In her view, staying married is not more important than the sanctity and safety of a woman.[1]

Catherine Clark Kroeger and Nancy Nason-Clark explain that when abuse is present, "Divorce is clearly the least desirable option, but sometimes it is a necessary option; and it is indeed a biblical option."[2] We have most likely heard ourselves and others randomly using the phrase "God hates divorce." It is a quote from Malachi 2:16. Catherine Clark Kroeger implores us to re-read the verse. "'I hate divorce,' says the Lord God of Israel, 'and I hate a man's covering himself with violence as well as with his garment,' says the Lord Almighty. So guard yourselves in your spirit, and do not break faith"(NIV). She goes on from this to ask why Christians do not think about other verses such as Proverbs 6:17–19 which lists seven other things that God hates: "haughty eyes, a lying tongue, hands that shed innocent blood, a heart that devises wicked plans, feet that hurry to run to evil, a lying witness who testifies falsely, and one who sows discord in a family."[3] She asks why the church compels victims to remain in marriages characterised by any of these qualities. It is too often the case that preservation of a marriage is exalted as a higher good than the safety of a human life. This is not what the Bible supports.[4] Her conclusion from this is that there is the possibility of a God-sanctioned divorce.[5] It is this possibility that should reinforce the serious nature of the offence and serve as an incentive for changing abusive conduct.[6]

Steven Fleming has worked in treatment centres for men who abuse and as a mental health specialist. Concerning the Malachi

---

[1] Carolyn Holderread Heggen, "Religious Beliefs and Abuse," 26.

[2] Nason-Clark and Kroeger, *No Place for Abuse*, 131.

[3] It should be noted that the NIV renders the last of these "hates" as "a person who stirs up conflict in the community."

[4] Nason-Clark and Kroeger, *No Place for Abuse*, 132.

[5] Ibid., 131.

[6] Ibid.

verse he says: "Those who speak out against divorce fail to read on. In the same verse God declares, 'And hate a man's covering himself with violence' (NIV). God considers both divorce and violence as evil. It may be argued at times violence can outweigh divorce as an evil, therefore justifying divorce as an act."[7] He agrees that divorce at times will be the lesser of two evils, and as such may be the answer to an unjust situation.[8]

As highlighted previously, Christian marriage is considered to be a covenant relationship. Some Christian women therefore face the dilemma of feeling compelled to remain committed to a marriage despite being victims of domestic violence. While divorce may not be a desirable option, it needs to be noted that covenants were established, broken, and renewed in the history of Israel. Together let's turn now to consider scriptures relating to covenants in the Bible.

Five issues have particular relevance:

1. Covenant scenarios in the Old Testament

2. The fact that covenants can be broken

3. The permanence of marriage

4. Covenant-making between individuals

5. The New Testament and divorce.

Covenant scenarios in the Old Testament

Old Testament scriptures describe the treaty arrangements of the nations and tribes among whom the Israelites settled. Making a covenant enabled two groups to define a relationship which allowed for responsibility and obligation. God adopted covenant principles in relation to his people. Catherine Clark Kroeger describes how at Mount Sinai the Israelites agreed to the covenant

---

[7] Steven R Fleming, "Competent Christian Intervention with Men Who Batter," in *Women, Abuse, and the Bible: How Scripture can be Used to Hurt or Heal*, ed. Catherine Clark Kroeger & James R Beck (Grand Rapids, Michigan: Baker Books, 1996), 183.

[8] Ibid.

whereby God set Israel apart from the other nations. This "set apart people" were to demonstrate to all other nations what it meant to serve God. In exchange God promised blessing, and to be their faithful God.[9]

Mitzi Eilts contributed a chapter in a workshop curriculum for clergy and helpers regarding domestic violence. She describes the mutuality of God's covenant—God makes promises and takes on responsibilities and, in addition, names the obligations required from the other partner to the covenant. "Covenants are good for us *and* good for God."[10] Contained within God's covenant were promises of deliverance, well-being, release from suffering, from persecution, or from being oppressed with an expectation of loyalty and "commitment of heart reflected in behaviour."[11]

Ron Clark talks of God establishing a covenant at creation (Genesis 2:15) and how a marriage relationship is similar in that the covenant is to be holy, calling for faithfulness from each partner.[12] Covenants with God have always been two-sided: "God promises to be faithful to humanity and expects the same loyalty from humanity. Since marriage is a reflection of a covenant between God and humans and between Christ and the church, loyalty within the covenant should reflect shared faithfulness."[13]

Nancy Ramsay is a Professor of Pastoral Theology and Pastoral Care. She says that there is an understanding that marriage is a covenant rather than simply a contractual arrangement. There is a difference in the expectation of trust within a covenant, and that care deepens the simple exchanges of a contract. A covenant marriage expects a context of mutual loving, honouring and cherishing.[14] Nancy Ramsay quotes Mitzi Eilts as follows:

---

[9] Nason-Clark and Kroeger, *No Place for Abuse,* 132.

[10] Mitzi N Eilts, "Saving the Family: When is Covenant Broken?" in *Violence in the Family: A Workshop Curriculum for Clergy and Other Helpers,* ed. Marie M Fortune (Cleveland, Ohio: The Pilgrim Press, 1991), 236.

[11] Ibid.

[12] Clark, *Freeing the Oppressed,* 82.

[13] Ibid.

[14] Nancy J Ramsay, "Confronting Family Violence and its Spiritual Damage,"

Covenants between people are reciprocal arrangements of care presuming mutually trustworthy commitments to particular obligations and responsibilities. There are consequences for not keeping faith in a covenant and repentance is necessary to restore the integrity of such agreements. Such vows make it clear that the spouse who abuses their partner is the one who breaks the covenant, not the one who leaves to assure self-protection and the protection of children.[15]

Covenants can be broken

"The scriptures leave no doubt that God's love always intends protection of the vulnerable so that divorce is preferable to continuing life threatening and dehumanising suffering for family members,"[16] says Nancy Ramsay. There are circumstances where a covenant is broken.

While God is loyal and faithful (see Deuteronomy 7:9–11 and Titus 1:2), God's people nevertheless violated the covenantal relationship (see Hebrews 8:7–13 and Jeremiah 11:8). God had two options as a response—to punish or forgive. God does both.

When Israel and Judah were captives of the Assyrian and Babylonian kingdoms, they turned their backs on God. God punished them by withholding compassion and protection and described the punishment as an abandonment or divorce:

Jeremiah 3:8 'I gave faithless Israel her certificate of divorce and sent her away because of all her adulteries. Yet I saw that her unfaithful sister Judah had no fear; she also went out and committed adultery."

Isaiah 54: 6–7 'The LORD will call you back as if you were a wife deserted and distressed in spirit—a wife who married young, only to be rejected," says your God. "For a brief moment I abandoned you, but with deep compassion I will bring you back." This is what the LORD says.

God had been faithful to Israel but they for their part had not been faithful to the covenant. Through the prophets God called

---

Family Ministry 20 (2006): 36.

[15] Eilts, "Saving the Family: When is Covenant Broken?" 240.

[16] Ramsay, "Confronting Family Violence and its Spiritual Damage," 36.

them to rectify their disregard, but the leaders chose to ignore God's requests for respect, loyalty, and love.

Ron Clark explains how the Israelites acted like a husband who ignores, abuses, or is unfaithful to his wife; and a wife who humiliates and is unfaithful to her husband. As such, the covenant relationship became dysfunctional. God was being humiliated and dishonoured because the people of Israel were being unfaithful (Isaiah 52:5; Ezekiel 36:22).[17]

God wanted to be loved and honoured among the other nations. God was worthy of respect as a God of love, truth, and mercy. In practising divorce, God was taking action to protect the purity and sanctity of the covenant with the people of Israel. It was they who brought dysfunctionality to the covenant relationship; it was the *people* not the covenant with whom God found fault. "God had to become over-functioning *(like an abused wife)* to keep the covenant, while Israel continued to under-function due to their sin and neglect *(like an abusing husband)*. God could not tolerate this kind of relationship and divorced Israel for the sake of the covenant. God punished them for the sake of honour. Divorce likewise, is an aggressive action to maintain the honour of covenant relationship."[18]

Ron Clark goes on and helpfully explains how marriage as a covenant is an agreement with obligations and stipulations and in addition, needs loyalty from each side. Loyalty relates not only to sexual faithfulness, but also to issues of respect and appropriate sharing of power. The covenant is violated when a spouse chooses not to honour, respect, and love the other. Divorce is not the problem, rather it is how one treats a spouse. Just as God has the option of calling bad behaviour to account, to expect repentance and request holiness, so too does a victim of abuse within a marriage.[19] So if you are in that reality as a woman experiencing abuse, you can name abuse for what it is and request accountability and change.

---

[17] Clark, *Freeing the Oppressed*, 83.

[18] Ibid., 84.

[19] Ibid.

In the case of Harriet, her loyalty was one-sided:

> I tried to get some support before I got divorced, because of the whole "covenant" thing. As a Christian, I wanted one marriage. I wanted one marriage partner. I wanted a way of making it better and making it right and tried to get some support at church before I got divorced. I thought, "I don't really want to get divorced if there's a way of saving the marriage," because I believed in the concept that it could, should, would be saved - that I had made a marriage commitment for life and this was the "better for worse" bit - that ultimately I am meant to work through whatever it is.

> I certainly had felt this strong sense of 'covenant' though. I think that's perhaps felt more because I am a Christian. (At the beginning), when I made my marriage vows, I was determined that there would be nothing that happened between us that we couldn't work out. As a loving couple, with Christian input in our lives, with children to keep us together and to give us a reason for being—I thought we would be able to work it out. Whatever came between us, we will be able to work it out.

> (Towards the end) I thought, "I don't know if I want to do it again and again and again. At what point do you decide you've done enough?"

The permanence of marriage

Catherine Clark Kroeger speaks to the claim that a marriage covenant must never be broken inviting us to note those instances where covenants have been broken between God's people and their God and what was the result. The covenant between Israel and God was described as a marriage which was betrayed and sabotaged by a wife who was idolatrous. Three times in the Old Testament there is reference to God divorcing his people (Isaiah 50:1; Isaiah 54:6–7; and Jeremiah 3:8). While not desirable, divorce was an option in particular situations. "The evangelical church cannot wholly condemn an action adopted by the Lord of heaven and earth in response to wilful and persistent sin."[20]

The language of blessing and curses within God's covenants is worth noting, especially as found in Leviticus 26:14–46, Psalm 78 and Deuteronomy 29. Such verses reveal that the consequences for breaking a covenant relate to being separated from God and God's favour. There are consequences when we don't keep our side of

---

[20] Nason-Clark and Kroeger, *No Place for Abuse*, 105.

the agreement and repentance is necessary for the covenant relationship to be restored. Look what God has to say here:

Deuteronomy 30:1–3 When all these blessings and curses I have set before you come upon you and you take them to heart wherever the Lord your God disperses you among the nations, and when you and your children return to the Lord your God and obey him with all your heart and with all your soul according to everything I command you today, then the LORD your God will restore your fortunes and have compassion on you and gather you again from all the nations where he scattered you.

2 Chronicles 7:14 If my people, who are called by my name, will humble themselves and pray and seek my face and turn from their wicked ways, then I will hear from heaven, and I will forgive their sin and will heal their land.

Ron Clark speaks of the negative reaction Christians have to the concept of God punishing or abandoning people. For some there is an expectation that God will be faithful regardless of our behaviour. God does not ignore unfaithfulness, neglect, and rebellion. While God promises faithfulness, God also expects reciprocal faithfulness. So can you. In a covenant relationship shared responsibility is a key feature. In Old Testament times, marriage was referred to as a covenant which was a common term for a binding agreement or contract. As such, a marriage contract as with any contract had within its arrangement agreement on penalties when or if the agreement was broken. Divorce and losing a dowry were the penalties for breaking a marriage contract.[21]

Ron Clark continues to explain how we know from the prophets that the Israelites and God were reconciled following separation. God initiated forgiveness and brought them back from Babylon. Once the nation repented (Daniel 9; Jeremiah 29) God renewed the covenant, bringing God's hope and peace in place of abandonment. God expressed mercy and grace in offering this new

---

[21] Clark, *Freeing the Oppressed*, 85, citing David Instone-Brewer, *Divorce and Remarriage in the Bible: The Social and Literary Context* (Grand Rapids, Michigan: 2002), 19.

start. God is clear, however, about expectations that the people were to be obedient and loyal in the covenant relationship.[22]

God wasn't saying you can do whatever you want. There were boundaries:

Zechariah 3:7 If you walk in my ways and keep my requirements, then you will govern my house and have charge of my courts, and I will give you a place among these standing here.

However, faithfulness is required from both sides for a covenant to be valid, and the consequences for breaking a covenant rest on the one who offends.[23] The person who is offended against has the right to choose forgiveness or punishment.[24] In breaking the covenant with God, Israel was forgiven many times. Nevertheless God punished and divorced Israel because, "the covenant had become dysfunctional" when the nation was audaciously violating the loyalty and trust given by God.[25]

These principles are transferrable to marriage; both partners are to be faithful with regard to the covenant. If abusive dysfunction dominates a marriage, both the covenant and spouse are at risk of being violated and dishonoured. The partner who is offended can choose to confront the offender and require repentance. The offender can choose to repent and commit to healing the relationship or risk being excluded and cut off from the marriage relationship.[26] An abusing husband has choices.

Just as there was provision for sacrifice to remedy sin, so too there was provision for divorce where there was an untenable situation (Deuteronomy 24:1).[27] Where a marriage is endangering family members, there needs to be careful consideration on the consequences of remaining in relationship. God's intention was to give meaning to life rather than to maintain a damaging

---

[22] Ibid.

[23] Ibid.

[24] Ibid.

[25] Ibid.

[26] Ibid.

[27] Nason-Clark and Kroeger, *No Place for Abuse*, 133.

relationship.[28] The welfare of children in divorce is an important consideration. If children within the family must endure the presence of violence, God's intent of covenant within marriage is violated.

Talking of her children Amanda says:

> There were lots of times—especially towards the end—when Jack would get angry with Tim and he'd push Tim into a corner, like the back door. And I physically pushed my way between Jack and Tim, so Jack wouldn't hit Tim. And I mean, there were times when I was frightened of him. It was aimed more at Tim than Louise, but I used to have to protect Mandy as well, when she was little. With Tim, Jack was threatening to punch him. Tim would've been seven. Jack just used to get so angry—just really, really angry. I preferred for me to get his anger, for his anger to be directed at me rather than to the kids. Because they were only little. Yeah, there were times when I did try to divert his anger towards me, and I used to defend the kids to the hilt. Defend the kids from him, protect them, especially Tim. He said to me years later after I left when we were talking one day, "Mum, I understand why you left." He said, "I know that Dad used to hurt you … Mum, you left it too long." He would have been about 12, but he knew what I'd gone through, he could see.

> But you stay together for the sake of the kids. I don't know why women think that. You stay together for the sake of the kids because you don't want the kids hurt. Well, my kids were hurting in the relationship. There was something on one of the DVDs I got from one of the kids' lawyers. It was about talking to children about separation, and how children feel about separation. There was one little boy who used to see fights between his Mum and his Dad. So to stop them from fighting with each other he would do something wrong so all their energy was towards him. So Mum and Dad weren't fighting anymore. When I listened to it and watched it for the first time, I thought, "That's what Tim used to do. That's exactly what Tim used to do". We were watching it together one day, and he said, "That's what I used to do—I used to try and cause a fight (directed at me) so you and Dad would stop fighting (with each other)." Which is sad, really, isn't it?

Ethel's children paid dearly as well:

> Actually my daughter was terrified of him I found out later, because of particular times that he had been really scary in how he administered physical punishment. It wasn't like it left physical scars on her, but it terrified her. And so for the rest of her life she will be on medication for anxiety because in her growing up and early teen years, anxiety was embedded because she did not feel safe at home. She was anxious that she was not physically safe. So you

---

[28] Ibid., 135.

don't have to beat somebody until they're black and blue—you can erode them, emotionally.

So why did I stay in it? Well, because after all, it wasn't like he was drunk, it wasn't like I was black and blue—and I made a sacred vow to love honour and cherish, until the day I died. "Till death do us part." Okay, it was a sacred vow. The only way I could actually get out of that one was by a blessing from the church—and the church wasn't recognising this. And people outside the church didn't understand the nature of that.

This was destroying me and my daughter, and he had already destroyed my son who had suicided in the midst of this—I mean, we're talking major impact. I can deal with the fact that I made a mistake and I was in a relationship that was not what I hoped—but dammit, what makes me really, really, angry was the cost to my children. As I said, my son lost his life, my daughter will be on medication for the rest of her life.

Regarding the church well dammit—they just wouldn't listen. It's about listening! You go in church and you sit down and you read the script and you sit and listen—I'm supposed to listen, but I'm not listened to. And the minister regurgitates all this and spits out a sermon that will be "one size fits all." But if I go and I ask for help then I'm given some band-aid like "It'll be okay," or "Oh you're just over-worried." They don't open it up and find out what's really going on.

So! Back to that often misused verse "'I hate divorce', says the LORD God of Israel, 'And I hate a man's covering himself with violence as well as with his garment'" (Malachi 2:16 NIV). Ron Clark explains that this does not imply God is angry toward those who are divorced; rather the text warns it is those who behave unfaithfully and violently who are provoking God's wrath. These scriptures in Malachi are about God calling his people back to relationship, and they challenge those who are being violent and dysfunctional in a covenant relationship to mend their ways. Yes, God hates divorce, but God will apply it where necessary, even though eager not to do so. What this reading of scripture suggests is that, contrary to the view of traditionalists, divorce is an option that can and should be exercised in an effort to maintain the covenant as holy and honouring.[29] Ron Clark reinforces the point: "While God accused Israel of sexual promiscuity (idolatry), God equally condemned them for social injustice and violence. Israel

---

[29] Clark, *Setting the Captives Free*, 86.

was divorced not only for idolatry but also for social injustice, violence and oppression (Isa 1:21–23)."[30]

Covenant-making between individuals

In the Bible there are many examples of covenants being established between individuals. This is seen in the relationship between Abraham and Abimelech (Genesis 20:14–16), and between Jacob and Laban (Genesis 31:44–54). And marriage is also clearly seen as a covenant between husband and wife.

Mitzi Eilts points out how the concept of marriage-as-covenant has historically been understood in two ways: first, as a mutual covenant between two people; and second, as a covenant offering protection or care in exchange for nurturing and/or obedience. The first of these most closely resembles and models God's purposes regarding marriage.[31] Where there is an agreement of exchange and obligation between humans (as in the second meaning), there is distortion and proneness to domination and control.[32]

Marie Fortune explains that there are four elements that enable a mutual marriage covenant which fulfils God's intention for relationship and most closely mirrors the covenant between God and people of faith.[33] These elements are:

1. It is made in the full knowledge of the relationship
2. It involves a mutual giving of self to the other
3. It is assumed to be lasting
4. It values mutuality, respect, and equality between persons.[34]

A marriage of this nature leaves little room or opportunity for abuse. Where it does occur however, promises and vows are broken and covenant trust is breached. When violence is occurring, the intent of the covenant is broken and the relationship becomes

---

[30] Ibid, 87.

[31] Eilts, "Saving the Family: When is Covenant Broken?" 238.

[32] Ibid.

[33] Ibid., 239.

[34] Ibid.

one of bondage and suffering rather than compassion, justice[35] and mutual loving.

This was a reality for Kiera:

> The first time we moved out. What brought me to it was his physical aggression, really. It came to a point—he was really violent. There was just no way we could be in the same house. At the time I remember he had the cricket bat, and he was just lashing out. There was just no way I could stay, or the boys. But yeah, that was the first time. Before that, there were times when I would stay away for a day because he was just in a very aggressive mood—we would stay away in a mall, just to be away and give him time to calm down. There was also a time it was very clear to both of us we were struggling in our marriage. About a month before we actually separated, I decided I wanted to go to my family for a month, just to be amongst people that appreciated me [chuckles] and loved me. And while I was away (this was how I explained it to my husband), we would both have time to think about what we wanted from our marriage, from each other, from how we see the future. And so I went. I took the children with me, and when I came back from my family he became very violent ...

> But you make this promise to stay ... Especially as we got married in a church too, and we made the promise before God and the people who were present, to stay "until death do part." And then you break a promise ... So it's quite... it's really huge. Somehow you need to work through that, because it's just that you've given your word, and now you take it back.

> And then there are your children, you see them—with all their pain, and their insecurities, and wounds that they carry around with them. And I mean, that's ongoing over years and years.

For the Christian woman caught up in such a situation, dilemmas inevitably occur regarding the marriage covenant. Her promises are important and significant, especially as they reflect a commitment to ensuring that the relationship will last. To stay may mean suffering but in leaving she feels she is breaking promises. Many do stay and suffer due to taking seriously their commitment but fail to comprehend that *the covenant is already broken by the abuse of the husband.*[36]

Mary's experience illustrates this ...

---

[35] Ibid., 240.

[36] Ibid., 241.

Covenant to me has always meant something really, really, very important, because covenant is something to be taken seriously. And I didn't think God ever broke covenants. So if we made a covenant with God, then we shouldn't break it either. Which sort of takes my mind down the road to—well, how bad is divorce then?

However, on the other hand, no one should have to put up with abuse—that's the other thing. But I think it would be hard for a woman to make that huge, huge choice ... This man isn't keeping the promises he made, so therefore it's got to be surely some way out ... in the godly sense. But I've never heard anyone say to me that that's how it could be.

Well, I was brought up thinking that marriage was forever—so that must've been instilled in me through my childhood. My parents were always together ... I can remember once or twice my father being a bit cruel to my mother. Once, I can remember (it's stuck in my mind like crazy—I don't know how it came about), but my mother was on the kitchen floor ... on the floor ... I was quite a small child—and she was crying and calling out, crying. And I don't know whether my father kicked her, but I can remember him being aggressive over her, angry, that's always stuck in my mind.

Eilts explains:

... throughout the scriptures, it is God or one called by God, (prophets such as Jeremiah, Isaiah, and John the Baptist) who calls attention to the fact that the covenant has been broken. It is God who says, 'If you want to be in a relationship with me you must change your ways—return to the promises you made with me.' God, is the one who has been faithful, is the one who says the covenant is broken; the covenant no longer stands. It is the one who has been faithful to the covenant who calls attention to the fact it has been broken, and that makes common sense does it not?[37]

The New Testament and divorce

In Matthew 5:27–32 and 19:3–9 we read of Jesus being questioned about an ongoing argument with the legalistic religious leaders. Some held the view that divorce was permissible when there had been adultery. Others believed that a variety of reasons could be drawn on to justify divorcing a wife such as burning the dinner or finding a more attractive or younger woman. Men often wanted to send their wife away but keep her dowry.[38] In Matthew 19:4–6, where Jesus defines marriage in terms of a one-flesh relationship,

---

[37]   Ibid., 238.

[38]   Nason-Clark and Kroeger, *No Place for Abuse*, 136.

he recasts adultery from being a property crime of one man against another, to the breaking of an important union which God created. In Jesus' view of marriage, a husband's unfaithfulness was a sin against a *wife*. In taking this stance, Jesus was recognising women as equal partners in the marriage relationship.[39]

When engaging in these debates the agenda for Jesus was not that abused women should stay with their husbands. Rather his concern was for misguided and misused male religious power. Carrie Miles comments that in relation to contemporary assumptions of the time regarding marriage and divorce, this was "a surprising twist."[40]

In this passage and in Luke 16:15–18, Jesus was responding to Pharisees who were seeking reasons and a validation for divorce, which often left women very vulnerable to exploitation. Jewish divorce had become influenced by the culture at the time, giving more freedom for men to divorce. Jesus' focus was not about forms or reasons for divorce. Rather he was making a stand to prohibit the common practice of men victimising their wives.[41] Nancy Ramsay says that while Jesus did speak against divorce, he nevertheless condemned men configuring options in their own interests thus allowing them to break sacred promises of care and leave divorced wives with few resources.[42]

Some people think that in Matthew 19 Jesus is saying adultery is the only excuse for divorce. According to Catherine Clark Kroeger divorce at this time was mainly initiated by husbands and options for women were limited. They could be given to another man or forced into prostitution.[43] In Matthew 5:32 and Matthew 19:9, however Jesus acknowledges that *porneia* was an allowable basis of divorce.[44] (It's important to understand that *porneia* is a broad term

---

[39] Carrie A. Miles, *The Redemption of Love: Rescuing Marriage and Sexuality from the Economics of a Fallen World* (Grand Rapids, Michigan: Brazo Press, 2006), 59.

[40] Ibid., 58.

[41] Clark, *Setting the Captives Free*, 86.

[42] Ramsay, "Confronting Family Violence and its Spiritual Damage," 36.

[43] Nason-Clark and Kroeger, *No Place for Abuse*, 137.

[44] Ibid.

that relates not only to adultery, but also to a variety of sexual deviancies such as abuse, fornication, inappropriate sexual attitude or action, and prostitution).[45]

The Bible offers two reasons women can seek divorce: unfaithfulness and desertion (see Matthew 5:32, Matthew 19:9 and 1 Corinthians 7:10–16). Author and Pastor Al Miles takes the view that where there is violence, the sacred vow of marriage, of oneness, is broken by an abusing husband. The abuser destroys a marriage covenant when he abuses his wife.[46] In essence, he "deserted" her by his inappropriate abusive behaviour.[47]

During my study it would often strike me, when listening to women's stories about long term abuse, that I would hear a lament: "I wish he would be unfaithful then I could justify a divorce." I want to make this really clear—ongoing abuse is a form of desertion. For women caught in the web of husbands with pornography addictions, these assertions are noteworthy.

Christian traditionalists claim marriage is a covenant in which a man and a woman make an oath before God and witnesses to stay together until death parts them. A couple make vows to honour, love, and respect and be faithful to each other. Paul speaks of this bond in Ephesians 5:21–33 and talks of mutual submission, comparing marital love to Christ's love for the church. The passage talks of a husband loving his wife as he loves himself and as Christ loves the church. Family violence stands outside these expectations for how followers of Christ should treat their family. Abuse disregards these instructions and disrespects Jesus and the church.[48] Al Miles says:

---

[45] Ibid.

[46] Al Miles, "Holding Christian Men Accountable for Abusing Women," in *Men's Work in Preventing Violence Against Women*, ed. James Newton Poling and Christie Cozad Neuger (Binghamton, New York: Haworth Pastoral Press, 2002), 20.

[47] Ibid., 20, Al Miles citing his own work in *Domestic Violence: What Every Pastor Needs to Know* (Minneapolis: Fortress Press, 2000).

[48] Ibid., 19.

Abuse also causes a great amount of damage to wives, children, and ultimately, to the abusers themselves because the perpetrators miss out on the many blessings God offers husbands and wives when both individuals commit to the biblical virtues of love and respect. Domestic violence is neither loving nor respectful, and … Christians must resist following the traditional pathway churchgoers take of labelling all marriages between Christians as holy.[49]

Al Miles continues and points out that many Christians hold the sanctity of a marriage covenant in higher esteem than the physical safety of women and children. A phrase which is often quoted is "a marriage must be saved at all costs." Therefore some women, despite ongoing violence, are told by pastors and counsellors to be obedient and prayerful and to remain in the relationship, believing that the marriage covenant is sacred and must not be broken.[50]

Celeste reflected on this:

The expectation was, well, marriage was … it was for life. You were expected to meet your vows and keep your vows—and regardless of what was happening, also as far as scripture is concerned—that divorce was hated; that God hates divorce.

Megan, for her part, commented:

I did go and get up the courage to finally talk to the minister's wife who had done a lot of counselling—so she was really "up there," and who I thought would be really sympathetic and practical … [sighs]. In the end (she had another elder come in with her), all they wanted to do was pray over me and encourage me to speak in tongues and stuff like that. I just thought—that's not what I want! I want practical help on what I can do in this situation. I was also quite frustrated. By the time I'd gone to talk to them the marriage had been in difficulty for a few years and we'd been struggling. I felt like I was doing all the hard work. But their attitude was, "Well you should just stick it out, because you don't want to give up on something that's been long-standing." And I thought, "Well, no … I'm not saying I want to give up, but I want to know how to get on."

I found it really hard to talk to Christian people about it, because I just had the impression that I was a failure as a Christian, as well as a woman, and a wife. So I tended to keep it pretty quiet. So that sort of situation went on and drifted on for quite a number of years, me feeling really horrible about the whole thing. Churches are so big on "family"—I did feel like a real failure,

49 Ibid., Al Miles is referring to his own work in *Violence in Families: What Every Christian Needs to Know* (Minneapolis: Augsburg, 2002), 19.

50 Ibid., 20.

twice the failure I would've felt out in the normal world where these sort of things happen and you deal with it and move on.

I think, because of the church thing and "marriage is supposed to be for life," I hung on and hung on and hung on and in hindsight I think I wasted ten years, where I should have called it quits a long time ago and said, "This is not going to improve." He wanted to stay married.

Saving the Family

Mitzi Eilts highlights the problem that occurs when emphasis is placed on saving a family by insisting on keeping the covenant despite the presence of violence in the relationship. Ongoing suffering often results. Victims sometimes stay patiently in a relationship in the hope that the relationship will get back to what it is intended to be. Choosing to be patient in such circumstances often reflects church teaching on long-suffering as a virtue.

However, long-suffering in response to what are seen to be God's ideals does not apply when suffering is imposed by one who has previously made promises to live with God's values for relationship but does not do so.

It is dangerous in an abusive relationship to apply hope and patience in the absence of safety and intervention, since the cycle of abuse will inevitably continue to worsen unless the abuser repents, takes responsibility and seeks assistance. A covenant relationship cannot be restored unless there is confession and repentance.[51]

Other Christian values lead to a victim tolerating abuse, such as when a woman feels guilty because of a belief that women are responsible for the quality of the marriage relationship. Because of this, some women think they deserve the treatment they are getting. However, "covenant is a two-way street, a partnership with responsibilities and obligations for both people involved ... Too seldom is the one who is really breaking the covenant, the abuser, being called to account for creating a home environment that is so oppressive that his partner needs to seek safety and peace elsewhere."[52]

---

[51] Eilts, "Saving the Family: When is Covenant Broken?" 240.

Amanda reflects:

> About God's will in my marriage—I always prayed that my marriage would get better. I always prayed that Jack would change, that my marriage would get better, that I could be the one that would change him ... and life would be different. Then I'd go back to "You made your bed and you lie in it."

> So I've made my bed and I'm lying in it—was this God's will for me?

Sadly, for some women separation from a husband will also mean judgement, separation, or expulsion from her church community. A victim seeking safety, separation, or divorce however, is acknowledging the marriage covenant is no longer operative, she is not the one breaking the covenant. While a marriage covenant is intended to last, scripture does not support a marriage suffering with violence. Nancy Nason-Clark and Catherine Clark Kroeger highlight that *it is violence which ends a relationship, not a victim's decision to leave.* A victimised wife does not necessarily bear responsibility for the failure of an abusive marriage.[53] As stated previously there are examples of covenants ending when their purpose has been ignored and transgressed. A marriage covenant is not more precious than the human being who is being wrongfully treated. The intention of a marriage covenant is to ensure that justice, mercy, and God's love are lived out and applied in ways consistent with a covenant.[54] When abuse cuts across this intention and ideal, a victim must be able to seek safety and peace, even if it means separation or divorce.

Amanda speaks of being ostracised by her church after leaving her abusive husband:

> The whole thing with leaving and divorcing in my marriage, I felt like it was (ongoing) abuse ... I guess it is abuse in a different way. I lived with an abusive husband in an abusive marriage, but then I left him. And then (I don't know if abuse is the word for it), but I was ostracised by people, I was ostracised by the church maybe. I was labelled. I felt like a leper. I thought people cared, but then when something like that happened, people withdrew from me. Did they really care for me in the beginning? Where's that unconditional love, you know?

---

[52] Ibid., 241.

[53] Nason-Clark and Kroeger, *Refuge from Abuse,* 51.

[54] Eilts, "Saving the Family: When is Covenant Broken?" 241.

That can be really hurtful too, because I've been through as much as I have, and all I wanted to do is start a new life, and I'd think that the people at church ... some of the people at church are your friends, and even my so-called friends don't want to know me. So I wondered how real the whole thing was at the beginning, really.

Conclusion

Hopefully these perspectives on marriage, covenants, and divorce give a bigger picture of God's compassionate heart. None of the Bible passages are intended as big sticks or rules to be held out to victims giving them no choice but to suffer. God would want none of this baggage imposed onto victims; God is lovingly on their side. The insights of these writers offer an invitation to look more comprehensively at the issues so that unnecessary spiritual baggage will be not imposed on abused women who are already weighed down .... As Jesus lovingly said, "Come to me, all you who are weary and burdened, and I will give you rest. Take my yoke upon you and learn from me, for I am gentle and humble in heart, and you will find rest for your souls. For my yoke is easy and my burden is light" (Matthew 11:28 NIV).

Chapter Five

Submission and Headship

Millie: Robert would often remind me (and the children) that he was the "head" of the household and that God had ordained this role for husbands. I struggled with this as it seemed to give him permission to be nasty, to be a bit heavy handed. He always had to have the last say. I didn't dare argue about some things—like the kids wanting us all to go and visit my parents. If Robert said no he meant no. Dad was a bit the same. Mum only told me recently that after she had my sister (her fifth child), she had gone on the pill and not told Dad, he would have been furious.

When I first got married I kind of wanted Robert to make all the big decisions about money, but I got tired of having to ask for small amounts and never being sure if he would say yes. Especially when it was for school uniforms, shoes, and the like. I wouldn't dare ask for money for anything extravagant for myself. He did give me a clothing allowance though, as he liked me to look good. It's not as if we were poor. He had a good job, a flash car. He went out with his mates on a Friday after work. And that new iPhone that was coming out, he would be getting it. He didn't want me to get a job. There was a part-time job going in school hours at the local homewares shop that would have been enjoyable. I am crafty and I could have made some money of my own. He said, "No, a wife's role is to serve her husband and children first and foremost and a working woman couldn't do that."

My father said to me when I got married, "Don't marry this man unless you're willing to come completely under his authority". But the Bible does say all that doesn't it? Wives are meant to be submissive. But I got tired of being under someone's authority. Actually he did some things which are not very God-like to me and the kids.

We are not together now. I have a trespass order which he has breached a couple of times. He still goes to church which means I can't go any more. My friend told me the church people feel sorry for him because I left him. But they won't know he hurt me one too many times. And I can't keep turning up at the women's refuge; the kids are getting too old for that now, my boy has turned 14. We are in the family court system working out access for the kids.

Is God disappointed with me?

Submission

In my experience, a dilemma for Christian women in abusive relationships is the belief that a dominant or leading role for the husband is God-ordained. At the same time these beliefs are seen by others to actually contribute to family violence. These principles are used to pressure women to stay in an abusive relationship. It's all wrapped up in Millie's questioning, "My father said to me when I got married, "Don't marry this man unless you're willing to come completely under his authority." But the Bible does say all that doesn't it? ....Wives are meant to be submissive."

The same claims (that the Bible says so), are also used by abusers to maintain and justify their behaviours.

Personally I get excited when an abused woman starts to question her abuse and her understanding of scripture. Hopefully she still believes that abusive behaviour is wrong. When the use of scripture is brought into the conversation there is an opportunity to ask her some questions. If his behaviour is wrong and hurting you and your children, how can it be coming from a sound use of scripture? If the messages, beliefs, and values in his head enable him to treat you badly, don't you want to give some consideration to questioning the accuracy of those beliefs? How come the same Bible which he thinks gives him permission to hurt you, tells him to live as a servant, to submit to you as well and love you to your potential?

Relationships of power, control, and abuse are neither what God created or intended. God, Jesus, and Paul went to great lengths to counter these unjust and violating demonstrations. In fact, *there is no room in God's agenda for women to be hurt through abuse.*

As previously said, often Christian women being abused understand various scriptures to mean that gender hierarchy was ordained by God at creation, and that this hierarchy is extended to marriage and family where husbands are assigned authority over their wives. Also within marriage, there are roles where the husband is the leader, the wife a submissive follower, and the spiritual welfare of the family is the husband's responsibility. Sadly these beliefs have been formed and shaped within church communities and these skewed beliefs do lead to women being hurt.

Both Amanda and her church leaders' understanding of scripture lead to her submitting to abuse:

Back in the Bible there were martyrs who submitted and were stoned for Christianity, and whose lives were taken ... Well, is what I went through with my husband part of suffering as a Christian? You know, like, my Mum used to say to me years ago (and I hate the saying), "You make your bed, you lie in it". I chose to do this and I had to stick with it.

My husband had an affair; our baby was six months old. Once he was angry with the dog and he threatened, "You wait 'til I get home, I'm going to fuckin' kill it; I'm going to fuckin' wring its neck." I was frightened. He would get angry with our son and push him into the corner and I would push my way between them, the kids were only little.

In my mind I'd go back to "You made your bed and you lie in it,"—so I've made my bed and I'm lying in it. If I hadn't had the kids I would have just killed myself for sure. The marriage never got better. One day I realised how unhappy I was and that I couldn't keep going like this anymore. But I felt like the church counsellors told me to stay. They insisted our marriage was sacred and meant to be permanent. "Let's try counselling, we'll try this and we'll try that, hang in there and everything will be alright, we'll pray for you"—I kind of felt I had a big, big weight, and all people wanted to do was pray. They had no idea the way that I lived. As for counselling, obviously, when you go to marriage counselling, you've got a husband and a wife together seeking help. You aren't going to be able to open up fully about how you feel, as I felt, with him being there, because you wouldn't feel safe. Because you can't feel safe, you can't let it all hang out, really, you can't open up and say exactly.

Filling the subservient role led to Kiera experiencing more abuse as she fitted in with her husband's demands:

Everything had to be focused around his life; life had to be fitted around his needs. In fact the more I tried to accommodate my life around his needs the more critical and blaming he became. I was constantly being blamed. It was getting too much.

Caught up in a similar situation, Celeste experienced an inability to protect her children:

He wanted to be the centre of attention, and did everything he possibly could to ensure he was. The result was that the children were neglected. The abusive behaviour—it wasn't just towards me, it was to the children and towards his Mum and siblings. Some of the things that happened I was horrified at.

Headship

Once again we will draw on the experts in the field of domestic violence towards Christian women. Nancy Nason-Clark refers to the work of Joy Bussert, explaining that as long as old-style religious traditions hold up submission as the ideal model for wife and husband relationships the battering of women will continue to be practised.[1] While there is an increasing awareness of such abuse within Christian evangelical books and magazines, "few are willing to confront the basic inequality of male-female relationships that is at the root of all forms of woman abuse".[2] Women in traditional marriage relationships where the husband is considered to be the "head" are beaten more often than women in egalitarian marriages.[3]

Researcher and psychologist Lenore Walker found that common characteristics of an abuser included holding fast to traditional ideas about family and roles, especially that the husband is the supreme leader in the home. As a result, he holds power and control in a domineering manner, believing that women are inferior and men superior.[4]

Ethel comments on her experiences of church culture that shaped behaviours:

> It was a theology of domination. The great God does all these things and is in control and takes charge—and that was mirrored by men being the ones who take charge, and they solve things by taking charge. Women are there to assist. Subservience and suffering are somehow virtuous in their own right.

---

[1] Nason-Clark, *The Battered Wife: How Christians Confront Family Violence*, 4.

[2] Shirley Gillett, "No Church to Call Home," in *Women, Abuse, and the Bible: How Scripture Can Be Used to Hurt or Heal*, ed. Catherine Clark Kroeger (Grand Rapids, Michigan: Baker Books, 1996), 110.

[3] Barbara Boone Wooten, *Destiny Denied: the Veiling of Women in the Traditional Church* (Lake Mary, Florida: Creation House, 2008), 73, citing Diana R Garland, *Family Matters* (Downer Grove, Illinois: Intervarsity Press, 1999), 200–201.

[4] Steven R Fleming, "Competent Christian Intervention with Men Who Batter," in *Women, Abuse, and the Bible: How Scripture can be Used to Hurt or Heal*, ed. Catherine Clark Kroeger & James R Beck (Grand Rapids, Michigan: Baker Books, 1996), 176.

[Leadership in church should be about] how we provide for children and marriages and things that help people grow instead of stamping them down and keeping them in line.

A big issue of course was sex. I was "being cruel" and depriving him of something that was really essential to him by not wanting to go to bed.

If we disagreed, who gets to decide? Well, he's the man, he's in charge, and I'm the woman. So how do we decide things? How important am I as a person and in fact, do I even own my body?

Megan highlights how the absence of women pastors in her church got in the way when getting help for the painful abuse of her husband's porn addiction. She would have liked to discuss these issues with a woman pastor:

A lot of pastors tend to be male, if you're in a small church and the minister's a male, you're limited.

My minister was interested in my situation. But if the issue being discussed did come back to sex, men see it differently from women, and well it was just uncomfortable talking about it with a man. Even on a practical sort of level, you know ... There had been issues in our marriage around pornography. Of course, pornographic stuff gives the husband an unrealistic expectation about what an ordinary, normal woman is about. It started to be that I couldn't "match up" (to those expectations).

There are differing views in churches about the role of women. Those with more traditional views claim the Bible teaches men were created to rule and dominate women. Some (Complementarians) believe men and women were created equal in worth but that God intends male and female to have different roles and functions. Others (Egalitarians) believe that God created men and women to relate as equals and that domination by men is a consequence of the Fall (when Adam and Eve sinned). Those who believe that the Bible teaches and supports equality, believe Jesus came to restore the relationship imbalance which was brought about due to the Fall.

The Bible does not support the idea of female submission and male headship. Rather, scripture endorses and teaches equal relationships between men and women, both in ministry and in marriage. As such, biblical misinterpretation and misrepresentation should not to be used to support, justify, or sanction abuse within the family.

Some thoughts on the attitude of male entitlement

The above discussion leads on to questions regarding the mindset of male entitlement. Such an attitude can contribute to abuse, especially where biblical misinterpretation plays a role in reinforcing mistaken understandings. These beliefs can influence perpetrators, victims, and those offering advice or help to the abused and the abusers.

Patriarchy describes a system of society or government in which men hold the power and women are largely excluded from it. Therapist Carolyn Holderread Heggen explains that the logic of patriarchy allows men the right to dominate and control their wives and families; it also allows the right to enforce control. It is this control over women and children that enables violent and abusive behaviours.[5] She refers to the authors Mary Helfer and Ruth Kempe who say in their book *The Battered Child*, "The assault rate on children of parents who subscribe to the belief of male dominance is 136 per cent higher than for couples not committed to male dominance."[6] Other concerns regarding the application of these values are raised by Lenore Walker's extensive research on battered women. Women with strong religious beliefs are the least likely to believe that the violence against them is wrong. Battered women also tend to hold to traditional views concerning sex roles in the home.[7]

Harriet's childhood and adulthood journey exemplifies these themes of the rights and expectation of male dominance:

> We were a "Catholic family." Until we got to teenage years—and by then Mum had been unwell, Dad had been in prison, the family was in a bit of a state. We sort of stopped being Catholic. I think because Mum went on the

---

[5] Carolyn Holderread Heggen, "Religious Beliefs and Abuse," 17.

[6] Ibid.

[7] Ibid., 18.

contraceptive pill—she had decided that was enough! So we didn't have that (ongoing church) involvement. But those beliefs I think follow you for a long, long time—that the church is in charge in some ways? I remember the priest coming in and looking around the house, sitting us down and giving Mum a bit of a hard time. Dad wasn't there, so the priest was in charge of the family—that's what it felt like. So we were very typically Catholic.

It is my biblical belief that my husband was supposed to love me like God loves the Church, and I'm supposed to be submissive or subservient or obedient. And I guess, deep down, I was looking for a stronger man than what I saw in my mother's and father's relationship. In actual fact, I married someone like my mother. I thought that my husband would make all the big decisions; I liked to think that I would be able to contribute. But I didn't originally see marriage as a partnership—I thought it was this sort of thing where he was more in charge. That was what I wanted.

I went through a stage of thinking that the marriage broke up because I contributed by disempowering him. Because I always worked, I always worked either part-time or full-time through our married life, even when the kids were little. I worked part-time and did nights—that was a financial reason as well. But also my mother was always so reliant on my father—she didn't have a profession, he earned the income and she stayed home with the kids.

I didn't want to be that dependent, and so I was fortunate enough to finish my nursing training and got to stay in the workforce, which meant I had financial freedom that my mother never had. Now I'm so grateful because I'm completely financially independent. But I did go through a stage—I still think there's a bit of me that wonders if I have contributed something to the breakup, because nothing is usually ever one person's fault. What he did was his fault, but what did I do that made him behave like that? I still struggle with what my role in it was I guess, although his behaviour is his behaviour. It's that whole idea that you're in it together, and "it takes two to tango" ... so I still have a bit of that stuff that I'm working through as well, I guess.

Carolyn Holderread Heggen is convinced that the Christian community cannot both support male entitlement and stop domestic abuse. Referring to Genesis 1–3, she says that patriarchy was not God's intention, but rather was a consequence of the Fall, a result of sin. We look to Jesus for the model for relationships which reflects values of the new creation. The revolutionary equality that was intended and instituted by Christ is seen in Ephesians 5:21–6:9 and Galatians 3.28: "There is no longer Jew or Greek, there is no longer slave or free, there is no longer male and female; for all of you are one in Christ Jesus" (NRSV).[8]

Other voices regard male entitlement as a dominant factor in abuse. A United Nations report on violence against women asks why gender violence continues seemingly unabated. The report says, "The answer is deceptively simple, but the solution is deeply complex: gender inequality fuels violence against women and the power balances it creates are not easily rectified."[9]

The report highlights a specific United Nations research project which looked into how the qualities of men are created and perpetuated and what it means to be a man in different cultural contexts. The focus of the research was to identify ways in which male violence developed and to find methods to rectify this.[10] Possible steps towards prevention identified in the report included addressing the larger context of violence.[11] Regarding Christian family violence, we need to be challenging how certain traditional beliefs around headship and submission contribute to the wider context of violence within Christian families.

A United Nations publication about ending violence against women claims: "There is no region of the world, no country and no culture in which women's freedom from violence has been secured".[12]

> The pervasiveness of violence against women across the boundaries of culture, race, and class points to its roots in patriarchy—the systemic domination of women by men.[13] The report claims violence against women cannot solely be attributed to individual psychological factors. To focus on individual behaviour or personal histories such as alcohol abuse or exposure to violence overlooks the broader impact and influence of long term gender inequality and its role in the subordination of women.[14]

---

[8]   Ibid., 19.

[9]   UNIFEM, "Not a Minute More: Ending Violence Against Women," 7.

[10]   Ibid., 70.

[11]   Ibid.

[12]   United Nations, *Ending Violence Against Women,* 28.

[13]   Ibid.

[14]   Ibid., 29.

Which Bible verses are used to support male entitlement?

There are some specific scriptures which have been traditionally used to argue for the subordination of women. Biblical scholar Craig Keener explores the specific nature of the original audiences to whom these verses were addressed. This helps us to understand what motivated Paul's instructions to the people he was writing to. This brief summary is drawn from his book, *Paul, Women and Wives.*[15]

One passage relates to head coverings and headship issues found in 1 Corinthians 11:2–16. Some claim Paul is insisting on women's subordination to men. Keener explains Paul is actually inviting the women in that particular situation to sacrifice their rights to dress in any way they might want to and to be considerate of onlookers who were observing the followers of Christ. If the Christian women were perceived as being inappropriate or extreme in their dress attire it was not going to be winsome for the new community of Christ followers. Christian women were being encouraged to be culturally sensitive with their choice of dress code so that non-believers would experience the new Christian community as more appealing than extreme.[16]

Of 1 Corinthians 14:34–35 where women in that context are told to be silent, some advocate that again Paul is supporting female submission. Keener tells us Paul was actually addressing uneducated women who were disrupting the services with irrelevant questions. Paul's remedy is for the women to stop asking the questions during the particular meeting times and be educated and informed in the long term.[17]

With regard to learning in silence in 1 Timothy 2:9–15, Paul is not claiming women should never teach, but that these particular women (who were unlearned) needed to learn before they could teach.[18] The important principle here is that no one, regardless of

---

[15] Craig Keener, *Paul, Women and Wives: Marriage and Women's Ministry in the Letters of Paul* (Peabody, Massachusetts: Hendrickson, 1992), 17.

[16] Ibid., 47.

[17] Ibid., 70.

gender, should be teaching inaccuracies or unhealthy interpretations of scripture.[19]

Keener explores Ephesians 5:18–33 and why Paul told wives to submit. Paul's social statements about equality between men and women were so radical at the time and contrary to cultural norms and he needed to be prudent.[20] He places wives submitting clearly in the context of mutual submission.[21] This was particularly progressive for this time.[22]

In considering the role of scripture and its negative contribution to domestic violence in promoting and reinforcing gender inequality, there are some principles worth noting. Catherine Clark Kroeger emphasises the challenge and value of fully understanding an ancient text in its original context in order to apply it appropriately to contemporary situations.[23] Abuse within the Christian home is often related to matters of biblical interpretation. Christians can both justify abusing and tolerate abuse using Bible verses. However, we need to discern what is descriptive about a time and situation in the Bible and what is prescriptive and meant for all time and situations. None of the above verses were intended by Paul to justify or support abuse.

Conclusion

Theologian Dr Gilbert Bilezikian explains how the first two chapters of Genesis describe God's ideal community on earth. Completely absent in the order of creation is a ranking structure between men and women. The original creation reflected oneness, mutual servanthood, and reciprocal submission.[24]

---

18 Ibid., 120.
19 Ibid.
20 Ibid., 139.
21 Ibid., 148.
22 Ibid., 139.
23 Nancy Nason-Clark, Catherine Clark Kroeger and Barbara Fisher-Townsend, ed., *Responding to Abuse in Christian Homes: A Challenge to Churches and their Leaders* (Eugene, Oregon: Wipf and Stock Publishers 2011), 8.

Until sin entered the world, harmonious co-operation between genders operated. The Fall had, and has, implications for domestic violence with regard to God's ideal being contaminated with qualities that were never part of God's original intention. These results are consequences of the Fall, and domestic violence is but one of the fruits.

We know Jesus came to reverse the negative outcomes of the Fall. As communities of faith, we are to live in ways consistent with God's ideal. Our marriage relationships provide an opportunity and invitation to live in the life-giving freedom of oneness and mutual interdependence modelled by Jesus in relation to God and the Holy Spirit. As Bilezikian says, "Whenever Christ is described as 'head' to the church, his ministry is that of servant-provider. Similarly, as head to his wife, a husband is a servant-provider of life, of opportunity and growth, not one who exercises authority over her."[25]

At the beginning of the chapter we reflected on the words of Millie who had endured abuse. Under the black cloud of believing submission was expected of her, she was never able to know the fullness of her own potential. We read the question from Ethel, who as an adult was asking, "Do I even own my own body?" Both these women had daughters who witnessed their abuse.

When an abused woman questions biblical claims about headship and submission there is hope. When responding, scripture must be used with integrity. Jesus didn't intend scripture to be the means of imprisoning a woman in an abusive relationship.

Jesus claimed the truth sets us free. He would say to Ethel, Millie, and their millions of sisters, "I came to bring life, life in all its fullness".

---

[24] Gilbert Bilezikian, *Beyond Sex Roles: What the Bible Says about a Woman's Place in Church and Family* (Grand Rapids, Michigan: Baker Academic, 2006), 171.

[25] Ibid.

Final Words to the Abused Woman

In the gospel of Luke, chapter 7, there is a small phrase said of Jesus as he notices a funeral and the plight of a poor widow. "When he saw her his heart went out to her" (Today's New International Version).

This phrase captures the longings I have in writing this book. Without doubt Jesus continues to see pain which is carried and hidden by Christian women affected by domestic abuse. Whether the abuse is in the present or past, the effects endure in various ways including relentless questions of faith.

Jesus not only sees, knows, and is present in your plight but is moved with compassion *for you*.

God's heart goes out *to you*.

It is my prayer that as you have read this book, you will experience Jesus inviting you to stop and rethink and reorient any false Christian beliefs you carry as a consumer of abuse.

You are not guilty for another's abusive behaviour, you are worthy of respect and safety. God doesn't require you to remain in an unrepentant and continuing abusive situation. In God's economy your safety, peace, and freedom from abuse and its effects are of great concern.

May your future choices be informed by truth and guided by wisdom. And may you experience in your choices God's compassionate heart, which goes out *to you*.

Bibliography

Acierno, R., H. S. Resnick, and D. G. Kilpatrick. "Health Impact of Interpersonal Violence: Prevalence Rates, Case Identification, and Risk factors for Sexual Assault, Physical assault, and Domestic Violence in Men and Women." *Behavioural Medicine* 23 (1997): 53–64.

Augsburger, David. *Caring Enough to Forgive.* 2 vols. Ventura, California: Regal, 1981.

Bilezikian, Gilbert. *Beyond Sex Roles: What the Bible Says about a Woman's Place in Church and Family.* Grand Rapids, Michigan: Baker Academic, 2006.

Blomberg, Craig. "On Building and Breaking Barriers: Forgiveness, Salvation and Christian Counseling with Special Reference to Matthew 18:15-35." *Journal of Psychology and Christianity* 25, 2 (2006): 145.

Bustanoby, Andy. "How do you Forgive the Unrepentant?" *Leadership* 12 (1991): 98–104.

Campbell, J. C. and K. Soeken. "Forced Sex and Intimate Partner Violence: Effects on Women's Risk and Women's Health." *Violence Against Women* 5, 2 (July 1999): 1017–35.

Campbell et al. "Assessing Risk Factors for Intimate Partner Homicide." *NIJ Journal* 250 (2003): 14-19.

Clark, Ron. *Freeing the Oppressed: A Call To Christians Concerning Domestic Violence.* Eugene, Oregon: Cascade Books, 2009.

Cooper-White, Pamela. *The Cry of Tamar Violence Against Women And The Church's Response.* Minneapolis, Minnesota: Fortress, 1995.

Donnelly, Doris. "Forgiveness and Recidivism." *Pastoral Psychology,* 33, 1 (1984): 15–24.

Eilts, Mitzi N. "Saving the Family: When is Covenant Broken?" Page 236 in *Violence in the Family: A Workshop Curriculum for Clergy and Other Helpers.* Edited by Marie M. Fortune. Cleveland, Ohio: Pilgrim, 1991.

Fleming, Steven R. "Competent Christian Intervention with Men Who Batter." Page 183 in *Women, Abuse, and the Bible: How Scripture can be Used to Hurt or Heal.* Edited by Catherine Clark Kroeger & James R. Beck. Grand Rapids, Michigan: Baker, 1996.

Fortune, Marie M. *Violence in the Family: A Workshop Curriculum For Clergy And Other Helpers.* Cleveland, Ohio: Pilgrim, 1991.

Freedman, L. "Wife Assault." Pages 41-60 in *No Safe Place: Violence Against Women and Children*. Edited by C. Guberman and M. Wolfe. Toronto: Women's Press, 1985.

Garland, Diana R. *Family Matters*. Downer Grove, Illinois: Intervarsity Press, 1999.

Gillett, Shirley. "No Church to Call Home." Page 110 in *Women, Abuse, and the Bible: How Scripture Can Be Used to Hurt or Heal*. Edited by Catherine Clark Kroeger. Grand Rapids, Michigan: Baker, 1996.

Haber, J. G. *Forgiveness*. Savage, MD: Rowman and Littlefield, 1991.

Heggen, Carolyn Holderread. "Religious Beliefs and Abuse." Page 27 in *Women, Abuse, and the Bible: How Scripture can be Used to Hurt or Heal*. Edited by Catherine Clark Kroeger & James R Beck. Grand Rapids, Michigan: Baker, 1996.

Heise, L., M. Ellsberg, and M. Gottemoeller. *Ending Violence Against Women*. Population Reports, Series L, No 11. Baltimore: John Hopkins University School of Public Health, 1999.

Holcomb, Justin S., and Lindsey A. *Is It My Fault? Hope and Healing for those Suffering Domestic Violence*. Illinois, USA: Moody, 2014.

Instone-Brewer, David. *Divorce and Remarriage in the Bible: The Social and Literary Context*. Grand Rapids, Michigan: Eerdmans, 2002.

Keener, Craig. *Paul, Women and Wives: Marriage and Women's Ministry in the Letters of Paul*. Peabody, Massachusetts: Hendrickson, 1992.

Millar, Melissa A. *Family Violence: The Compassionate Church Responds*. Waterloo, Ontario: Herald, 1994.

Miles, Carrie A. *The Redemption of Love: Rescuing Marriage and Sexuality from the Economics of a Fallen World*. Grand Rapids, Michigan: Brazo, 2006.

Miles, Al. *Domestic Violence: What Every Pastor Needs to Know*. Minneapolis: Fortress. 2000.

———. "Holding Christian Men Accountable for Abusing Women." Page 20 in *Men's Work in Preventing Violence Against Women*. Edited by James Newton Poling and Christie Cozad Neuger. Binghamton, New York: Haworth Pastoral, 2002.

———. *Violence in Families: What Every Christian Needs to Know*. Minneapolis: Augsburg, 2002.

Moule, C. F. D. *Forgiveness and Reconciliation: Biblical and Theological Essays*. London: SPCK, 1998.

Nason-Clark, Nancy. *The Battered Wife: How Christians Confront Family Violence*. Louisville, Kentucky: Westminster John Knox, 1997.

Nason-Clark, Nancy, and Catherine Clark Kroeger. *No Place for Abuse: Biblical and Practical Resources to Counteract Domestic Violence.* Downers Grove, Illinois: Inter-Varsity Press, 2001.

————.*Refuge from Abuse: Healing and Hope for Abused Christian Women.* Downers Grove: Inter-Varsity Press 2004.

Nason-Clark, Nancy, Catherine Clark Kroeger, and Barbara Fisher-Townsend, eds. *Responding to Abuse in Christian Homes: A Challenge to Churches and their Leaders.* Eugene, Oregon: Wipf and Stock, 2011.

Quillan, J. P. "Screening for Spousal or Partner Abuse in a Community Health Setting." *Journal of the American Association of Nurse Practitioners* 8 (1996): 155–60.

Ramsay, Nancy J. "Confronting Family Violence and its Spiritual Damage." *Family Ministry* 20, 3 (2006): 36.

Schweitzer, Carol L Schnabl. "Violence Against Women and Children: How Churches Can Respond." *Word and World* 24, 1 (2004): 69.

Smedes, Lewis. *Forgive and Forget: Healing the Hurts We Don't Deserve.* New York: Harper Collins, 1984.

————. "Forgiving People Who Do Not Care." *Reformed Journal* 33 (1983): 13–18.

Stark, Evan and Anne Flitcraft. "Medical Therapy as Repression: The Case of Battered Women." *Health and Medicine* (Summer/Fall 1982): 32.

————."Violence Among Intimates: An Epidemiological Review." Pages 293-317 in *Handbook of Family Violence.* Edited by Haslett et al. New York: Springer, 1987.

"Statistical Report 2014-15." https://womensrefuge.org.nz/wp-content/uploads/2015/11/Domestic-violence-statistics-NZ.pdf

" Statistics." http://areyouok.org.nz/family-violence/statistics/.

Straus, Murray. "Ordinary Violence, Child Abuse and Wife Beating: What Do They have in Common?" Pages 403-24 in *Physical Violence in American families.* Edited by Murray Straus and Richard Gelles. New Brunswick, NJ: Transition, 1990.

Tracy, Steven R. "Patriarchy and Domestic Violence: Challenging Common Misconceptions." *Journal of the Evangelical Theological Society* 50, 3 (2007): 573.

————."Sexual Abuse and Forgiveness." *Journal of Psychology and Theology* 27, 3 (1999): 220.

UNIFEM. "Not a Minute More: Ending Violence Against Women." New York: United Nations Development Fund for Women, 2003.

United Nations. *Ending Violence Against Women: From Words to Action*. Edited by Secretary General. New York, USA: United Nations, 2006.

Wooten, Barbara Boone. *Destiny Denied: the Veiling of Women in the Traditional Church*. Lake Mary, Florida: Creation House, 2008.

World Health Organization. *World Report on Violence and Health*. Geneva, Switzerland: World Health Organization, 2002.

Appendix

The thesis, also called "Dishonoured and Unheard: Christian Women and Domestic Violence" can be found on www.projectesther.co.nz or can be sent by email from daphnesgracie@hotmail.com. The thesis was part of a Master of Theology with Laidlaw College New Zealand.

Lightning Source UK Ltd.
Milton Keynes UK
UKHW010616061219
354841UK00003B/849/P